Official American Mensa Puzzle Book

THE LITTLE GIANT® ENCYCLOPEDIA OF *Mensa Mind Teasers*

Edited by Peter Gordon

Sterling Publishing Co., Inc.
New York

Library of Congress Cataloging-in-Publication Data Available

2 4 6 8 10 9 7 5 3 1

Published by Sterling Publishing Company, Inc.
387 Park Avenue South, New York, N.Y. 10016
This book is compilation of excerpts from the following Sterling titles:
Mighty Mini Mind Bogglers by Karen C. Richards © 1999
Mighty Mini Cryptic Crosswords by Henry Hook © 2000
Mighty Mini Rhyming Picture Puzzles by Steve Ryan © 2000
Mighty Mini Crypto-Quotes by Leslie Billig © 1999
Mighty Mini Crosswords by Trip Payne © 1999
101 Checker Puzzles by Robert Pike © 2000
Nearly Impossible Brain Bafflers by Tim Sole & Rod Marshall © 1998
Ingenious Puzzles for Word Lovers by George Bredehorn © 2000
Quick-to-Solve Brainteasers by J.J. Mendoza Fernández © 1998
Hard-to-Solve Brainteasers by Jaime & Lea Poniachik © 1998
© 2001 Sterling Publishing Co., Inc.
Distributed in Canada by Sterling Publishing
c/o Canadian Manda Group, One Atlantic Avenue, Suite 105
Toronto, Ontario, Canada M6K 3E7
Distributed in Great Britain and Europe by Cassell PLC
Wellington House, 125 Strand, London WC2R 0BB, England
Distributed in Australia by Capricorn Link (Australia) Pty Ltd.
P.O. Box 6651, Baulkham Hills, Business Centre, NSW 2153, Australia

Sterling ISBN 0-8069-0155-1

CONTENTS

Introduction   5

Mind Bogglers   7

Cryptic Crosswords   43

Rhyming Picture Puzzles   85

Crypto-Quotes   133

Crosswords   177

Checker Puzzles   219

Brain Bafflers   255

Puzzles for Word Lovers   275

Quick-to-Solve Brainteasers   315

Hard-to-Solve Brainteasers   349

Hints   381

Answers   387

Index   510

INTRODUCTION
•••••••••••••••••••••••

This book is a veritable smorgasbord of puzzles. No matter what your tastes are, you'll find at least a few delicious puzzle types to enjoy. You can choose from crosswords, cryptics, Two By Twos, picture puzzles, brainteasers, checker problems, cryptograms, and more. If, when you're finished, you have a few left-overs that aren't your favorite puzzle flavor, pass the book on to a friend. I'd hate to see a good puzzle go unsolved. Bon appétit!

—Peter Gordon

Mind Bogglers

Karen C. Richards

Answers on pages 388–395

Mind Boggler

Here's a quick brainteaser: What is special about the grid below—and what is missing from it?

Answer, page 391

U	R	O	W
O	N	G	T
F	I	E	H
X	V	S	R

Tying the Knot

According to an ancient custom, if a woman throws five ropes out of a high window, and three or more of them land such that they will form knots when both ends are pulled, she will be married within the next year.

The ropes here show one woman's tosses. Should she expect a wedding this year?

Answer, page 395

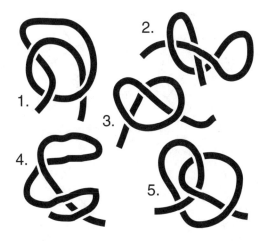

Technique-Color

Jo is making a stained-glass window, and she wants each adjacent piece of glass to be a different color. She wants to use just four colors: yellow, orange, purple, and red.

If the center circle is yellow, and two other pieces are colored as shown, what color does piece A need to be?

Answer, page 393

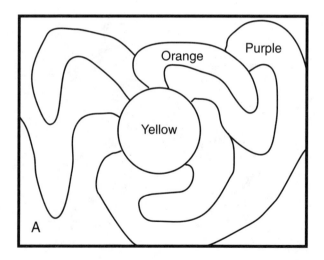

Animal Strength

If the first two tug-of-war contests shown here are ties, which group will win the third contest, or will it also be a draw?

Answer, page 388

Theory of Relativity

At the Embee family reunion, your sister is talking to your grandmother Mary, your cousin Bo, and your uncle Bill. Who are you?

Answer, page 394

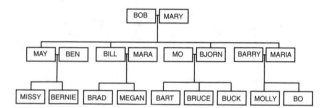

Paper Clip Flip

Most of the wire sculptures below were made from standard paper clips, by twisting them at existing bends.

Which of the shapes could not have been made by bending the original paper clip?

Answer, page 392

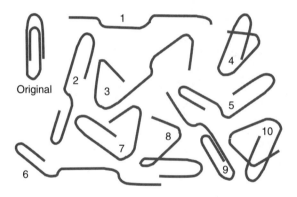

Original

12-Step Program

Work through the code of this computer program, line by line. Your output will answer this riddle: WHAT DID COWBOY DAVE HAVE TO DO BEFORE GOING TO THE COMPUTER-USERS' DANCE?

```
01 Set Number = 1
02 Set Letter at (Number) = "P"
03 Number = Number + 3
04 Set Letter at (Number) = "O"
05 Number = Number + 1
06 If Number ≤5 go to line 04
07 Set Letter at (Number) = "B"
08 Number = Number ÷ 3
09 Set Letter at (Number) = "U"
10 Number = Number + 1
11 Set Letter at (Number) = "T"
12 Reverse the output
```

Output:

‾‾‾ ‾‾‾ ‾‾‾ ‾‾‾ ‾‾‾ ‾‾‾
 1   2   3   4   5   6

Answer, page 395

Thirteen Candles

Claude doesn't want anyone to know how old he is unless they do some work. So he designed a birthday cake that uses 13 candles and represents his age.

If you count all of the triangles of all sizes formed by the lines connecting the candles, you will discover Claude's age. Can you figure it out before the candles are blown out?

Answer, page 394

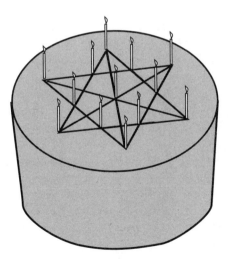

15

Hairy Tales

1. Rapunzel's hair grew 100 feet longer while waiting to be saved by the prince. Hair grows one inch every two months. So, how long had the fair maiden been trapped in the tower when she was rescued?

2. In Washington Irving's story, Rip Van Winkle's beard grew two feet in the 20 years that he slept. Is the story accurate?

Answer, page 391

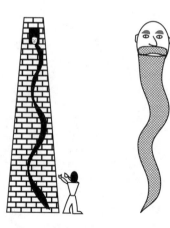

Keep the Faith

The eruptions of the Old Faithful geyser are indeed very predictable. Below are the last five eruptions:

1. at 12:00 P.M. for five minutes
2. at 12:50 P.M. for six minutes
3. at 1:44 P.M. for seven minutes
4. at 2:42 P.M. for eight minutes
5. at 3:44 P.M. for nine minutes

Can you calculate when the next eruption will be?

Answer, page 391

Block Party

The alphabet blocks below are of two different types, turned around in various positions. No letter appears on both types of block. The letters on the underside of the blocks spell out the answer to this riddle:

HOW DID BARBIE GET THROUGH THE PILE OF ALPHABET BLOCKS?

Can you do some mental tumbling and figure out the solution?

Answer, page 389

She took the . . .

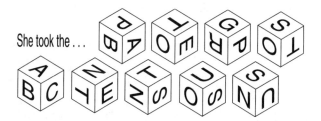

Self Test

The answers to the questions below are one-digit numbers from one to nine, and no number is repeated. Can you figure out the unique set of answers?

1. Answer to statement 5 minus answer to statement 4.
2. Answer to statement 8 times answer to statement 9.
3. Answer to statement 4 plus answer to statement 8.
4. Number of times that the number 9 is an answer.
5. Total number of statements.
6. Answer to statement 1 minus answer to statement 4.
7. Number of odd answers.
8. Answer to statement 2 divided by answer to statement 9.
9. Answer to statement 6 minus answer to statement 7.

Answer, page 392

19

Losing Track

On this animal track quiz, one student copied his or her answers from the other three students. By looking at their answers below, you should be able to tell who cheated.

Ironically, the cheater got none of the answers correct. If the other students had two correct answers each, what are the correct answers?

The Question:
Match these five tracks to the animals that made them.

The Answers:
ART: 1. deer 2. caribou 3. mt. goat 4. moose 5. bison
BOB: 1. caribou 2. moose 3. deer 4. bison 5. mt. goat
CAT: 1. bison 2. mt. goat 3. deer 4. caribou 5. moose
DEB: 1. deer 2. moose 3. mt. goat 4. caribou 5. bison

Answer, page 391

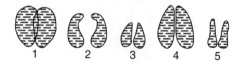

Blind Alleys

On his birthday, Joe's friends blindfolded him and took him for a drive.

If they took two right turns, a left turn, and another left, and ended up at Wally World, where did they start?

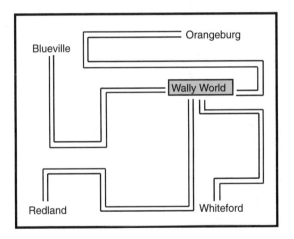

Answer, page 388

Graphic Language

Find the letters that correspond to the coordinates given below. Write them in order on the dashes to answer this riddle: WHY WAS SIX AFRAID OF SEVEN?

1. C5
2. G3
3. A3
4. D5
5. F2
6. A1
7. D2
8. F4
9. B4
10. E6
11. B6
12. C3
13. A5
14. E1

6	D	N	R	Y	T	M	F
5	N	L	S	E	O	K	Z
4	P	H	J	C	B	G	A
3	V	O	I	R	U	W	E
2	U	M	X	I	T	N	P
1	E	A	G	Q	E	S	L
	A	B	C	D	E	F	G

Answer:
BECAUSE __ __ __ __ __ __ __ __ __ __ __ __ __ __

Answer, page 390

Produce Products

The numbers one through nine are represented by nine different vegetables in the equations below. Each veggie represents the same number throughout. If the broccoli equals three, what is the identity of the carrot?

Answer, page 392

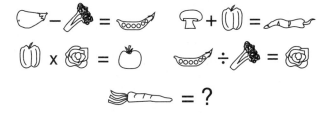

What's the Plan?

Which three-dimensional object at the bottom does the simple orthographic projection above it represent?

Answer, page 395

TOP

FRONT

RIGHT SIDE

1.

2.

3.

4.

5.

Fraction Words

Add the parts of words below as indicated to come up with two answer words. In each case, use the first letters of the word in your addition. For example, one-third of CAT would be C.

Both solutions answer this riddle: What has keys, but can't open a door?

Answer, page 390

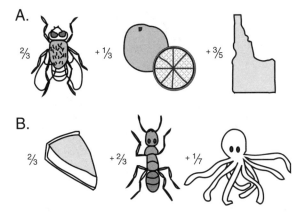

A.

$\frac{2}{3}$ $+ \frac{1}{3}$ $+ \frac{3}{5}$

B.

$\frac{2}{3}$ $+ \frac{2}{3}$ $+ \frac{1}{7}$

Three Hexes

Most of the shapes here can be made by combining three equal-sized hexagons. Which ones cannot?

Answer, page 395

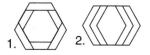

1. 2.

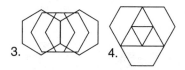

3. 4.

5. 6. 7.

Ten Gold Coins

Ten gold coins are hidden under ten of the unlabeled hexagonal tiles in this floor. The numbers on the labeled tiles indicate how many coins are under tiles adjacent to that tile.

Can you locate the ten gold coins without looking under any of the wrong tiles?

Answer, page 394

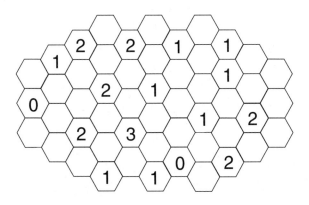

Mirror Images

Using only a square mirror and the jigsaw shape below, most of the figures below can be formed. Which figures are impossible? (Remember, parts of the new shapes are seen in the mirror.)

Answer, page 392

Winter Eyes

To make simple snowflakes, fold a square of paper into quarters, cut shapes, and unfold. Which folded snowflakes (1–7) will unfold to create snowflakes A, B, and C?

Answer, page 395

Fishing for Words

Remove words from the nonsense paragraph below as instructed. When you are done, the words that remain will spell out a Spanish proverb.

THOUGH FEROCIOUS THE GREEN TURTLE SPIT LOWER FISH STRESSED BARREL DIES GULP BECAUSE HE EAR CANNOT PLUG OPENS RIGHT INK HIS TEN WHISTLING TIPS SHARKS NET MOUTH LAKE DESSERTS.

1. Remove all of the words that are between two words that begin with a T.

2. Take away all of the pairs of words that spell each other backward.

3. Cross out all of the words that become another word when an F is added before the first letter.

4. Remove all of the six-letter words.

Answer, page 389

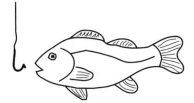

Got Class?

It's time to put together your class schedule for next semester's classes. You need to take two science classes, one math or computer class, one English class, and one history. Given the list of classes that sound interesting to you, which combination of class times will work? (R is Thursday.)

American history	TRF 9:05–10:00
Biology	TR 8:00–10:00
Calculus	MW 11:15–1:15
English lit	TR 9:05–10:00
European history	MWF 10:10–11:05
Genetics	MWF 12:20–1:15
PC basics	TR 12:20–1:15
Physics	MWF 10:10–11:05
Shakespeare	TR 11:15–1:15
Statistics	MWF 8:00–9:10

Answer, page 390

Next in Line

The four pictures below form a logical sequence in order from left to right. Can you figure out what links one picture to the next and then deduce which of the three objects (a, b, or c) below comes next in the line?

Answer, page 392

1.   2.   3.   4.

a.

b.

c.

Match Boxes

Which pieces of cardboard below will form boxes if they are folded along the lines?

Answer, page 391

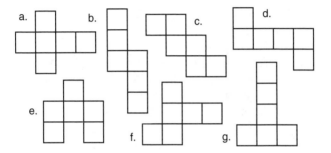

A Good Egg

Ostriches lay the largest eggs in the world. To find out how many omelets can be made from one ostrich egg, solve the word puzzle below. (Each omelet uses the equivalent of two hen's eggs.)

Spell the six-letter answer as described:
1. A letter in EGRET but not GREBE
2. A letter in CROW but not CONDOR
3. A letter in WARBLER but not BARN OWL
4. A letter in KESTREL, EAGLE, and FALCON
5. A letter in RAVEN but not CRANE
6. A letter in PIGEON, WREN, and OSPREY

— — — — — —

Answer, page 390

Sea or Soil?

The good news is that your rich uncle Charlie has bequeathed to you a treasure map. The bad news is that it has been ripped on all four sides, so that you have only the key piece.

You are told that there is a treasure buried at point X and that point A is on land. If the area is composed of one lake and the land around it, and there are no islands in the lake, is the treasure undersea or under land?

Answer, page 392

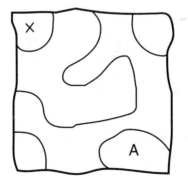

Berry Impressive

A new, genetically engineered strawberry clones itself every month, except for the first month, when it is dormant. Each new strawberry is identical to the first one in that it, too, clones itself every month after being dormant for a month. If one of these new strawberries is planted at the beginning of March and harvested at the beginning of November, how many berries will result?

Answer, page 388

Fishing Lines

Today, eight people are trying to hook some trout on this part of the Lazy River.

Fishermen like to fish their own holes. To separate everyone, draw two straight lines across the map so that each fisher is on his or her own piece of river. Can you find a way for Mac to fish on his own piece of river? What about Bill?

Answer, page 389

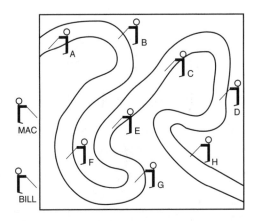

Ages of Reason

Aunt Pearl doesn't like to tell anyone her age, but she will say this:

"In Roman numerals, my age is made up of one I, one V, one L, and one X. My age is the second largest number that can be made from those symbols. My daughter's age is the second smallest number that can be made from those symbols."

How old is Pearl and how old is your cousin?

Answer, page 388

Black and White

In this game, you can see your friends' cards, but not your own. If there are four black cards and four white cards to choose from, can you deduce which cards you have by what the other players know?

Answer, page 388

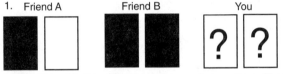

1.   Friend A   Friend B   You

Neither Friend A, Friend B, nor you know what you have. Then, friend A says she knows. What cards do you have?

2.   Friend A   Friend B   You

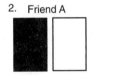

Neither Friend A, Friend B, or you know what you have. Then, Friend A still doesn't know. What cards do you have?

Slice of Life

Your meatball pizza just came out of the oven and now you need to feed six hungry kids. These kids are picky, so they each want the same number of meatballs. They also each want the same size piece of pizza. How can you cut the pie to satisfy all six kids?

Answer, page 393

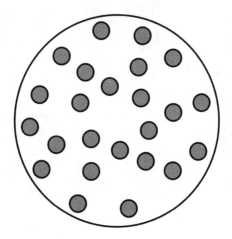

For Your Thoughts

1. Which circle below is the size of a penny?

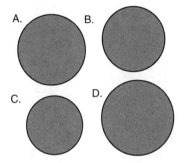

A.
B.
C.
D.

2. How many pennies, stacked on their sides, equal the diameter of one penny?

A. eight B. ten C. twelve D. fourteen

Answer, page 390

Game Plan

In these super tic-tac-toe games, the letters are entered from the top of the board, so that only the lowest empty box in each column can be played. If it's O's turn in game A and X's turn in game B, who should win each game? (Three X's or O's in a row wins.)

Answer, page 390

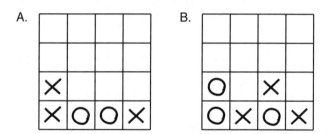

Cryptic Crosswords

··

Henry Hook

Answers on pages 396–405

ACROSS

1 Weaklings whomped on the head by pranksters (5)

4 *The Fleet's In* based on a true story initially (5)

7 One in unending sex story (11)

8 Eccentric officeholder trapped by recession of Y2K (5)

9 New Christmas song describes peace symbolically (5)

10 Secretly search front of boat near lake (5)

12 Beer ingredient found at a Mediterranean island (5)

14 Orator following lines of French lawgiver (11)

15 Tree of greater age (5)

16 Expert in a Cabinet division (5)

DOWN

1 Finish off corn liquor with a quick stroke (5)

2 Monsieur replaces me before Democrat is led astray (11)

3 Oversentimental agent holds middle of rope (5)

4 Nobleman in tavern, performing (5)

5 Overcome by the prevailing mood, Valerie shows uncertainty (11)

6 Enlarge small hole in the ground (5)

10 Chaplain quietly read *Mad* (5)

11 Firm from the south carries small, futuristic weapon (5)

12 Those people boosted a symphony conductor (5)

13 Review of Polanski movie: A plus (5)

1

Answer, page 396

ACROSS

4 Judges are almost stung by charges (10)

6 Announced greatness of Greek characters (4)

7 Red pen's point returned with notebook (6)

8 Unusual headers in *Rock and Roll Encyclopedia* (4)

9 Execute witch around back of cauldron (4)

12 Dress that man after Mass (6)

14 Hotels selected by Nova Scotia (4)

15 Fellow judge in Los Angeles outlaws people from Winnipeg (10)

DOWN

1 Someone mistreating a coach on TV medical drama (6)

2 Little soldier's face concealing a hint of worry (4)

3 Powdered soaps discourage men (10)

4 Alberta's premier and American to tack pictures up for Ozzie? (10)

5 Bust plastic margarine containers (4)

10 Going north, Asian monk takes in beast (6)

11 Raise one thousand dollars for gambling game (4)

13 Hear story end (4)

Answer, page 396

ACROSS

1 Tell about metal, smooth and lustrous (6)

5 FYI: Traveling around France's capital is doubtful (4)

7 I have to chase Jack's kid (4)

8 State, "Letterman's back in North America" (6)

9 Commotion behind us (6)

10 Hillbilly's caught sight of offspring? (4)

11 I study a picture (4)

13 In Spain, 1¼ dozen fruit (6)

15 Invader sheltered by Patti LaBelle (6)

16 Admit nothing in a Volkswagen (4)

17 Hole in that woman's footwear (4)

18 Male or female imp, twisting, shows nonrigidity (6)

DOWN

2 Leader of union, supporting radical idea, is leaving word? (5)

3 Popular old partner, thoughtful and reasonable (11)

4 Americans can be such jerks (5)

5 Explore rear half of cave, overcome by urge (11)

6 Tamper with candy (5)

12 Trap lion or tiger with pair of chains (5)

13 Drink quart right off, very loudly (5)

14 The end is near (5)

Answer, page 397

ACROSS

1 Add alcohol left by pilot (4)
3 Ex-builder (6)
7 Surly Republican involved in foolish talk (5)
9 Contaminated draft animal overcome by spasm (5)
10 Very small bat in Finland heading to cave (9)
12 Actress Annette consumes liquor, for a start (9)
16 Linked with an urban area in either direction (5)
17 Composer from South America (5)
18 Only one line for big star on the Riviera (6)
19 A monarch, but not quite related by blood (4)

DOWN

1 Band behind record company's symbol (4)
2 Successful strokes put ball in holes, in golf (5)
4 Passes nuts to us on journeys (9)
5 Saw mother returning potpourri (5)
6 Ornate red disc seen by Ms. Chanel (6)
8 Story about a group watching trucks repulsed mathematician (9)
11 Air conditioner installed in a jitney? Count on it (6)
13 Did Grant pound small mallet? (5)
14 Composer's good fortune (5)
15 *Roll Over Beethoven*'s ending when the sun comes up (4)

4

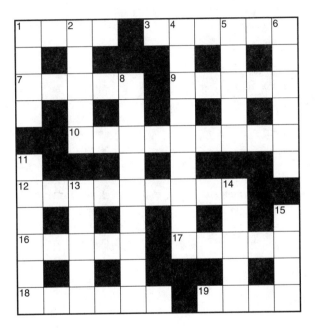

Answer, page 397

ACROSS

1 Electronic lines on screen in quick examination (4-4)

7 Enthusiastic opera singer making a comeback (4)

8 Salted crackers kept for a long time (6)

9 A deadly sin? Yes (6)

10 Mountain beast still accompanies one (4)

11 Hero penning *Beginning of the End*? (4)

13 Actively purchase about 50% silver (6)

15 Owner's new sink (6)

16 Scourge of up-to-date radio station? (4)

17 E.g., dinner for winner of mile run? (8)

DOWN

2 Plotting a course, having a great interest in land (10)

3 Give a gift to university in need of renovation? (5)

4 Well-founded Vidal novel (5)

5 Not safe in Rhode Island? Heavens! (5)

6 Big number before 10 in ESPN broadcast (10)

12 Head of state's invested in boom or bust (5)

13 Coach takes on something extra (5)

14 Small pitcher—a vessel for dirty water? (5)

5

Answer, page 398

ACROSS

4 Franchised to play for the Devils (10)

7 River plant (6)

8 Home by the Fourth of July? Say it isn't so (4)

9 Top copy for adults only (4)

11 Back with green pond creature (4)

13 Metal zipper's front, ¾"? (4)

14 Rush swallows a cheer (6)

16 A *Sports Illustrated*, with cover that's smooth, is influential (10)

DOWN

1 Friend twisted back—I have relief (10)

2 Boat from South Jersey (4)

3 Kind nurse (6)

5 Cook has initially unleashed anger (4)

6 Spoke disparagingly of Greek tenants held up (10)

10 Tax cut (6)

12 "Bird indigenous to Madagascar," he added (4)

15 Nearly repentant about devastation (4)

6

Answer, page 398

ACROSS

1 Ace wearing muffler is back in fight (6)
5 Bring bad luck to Jack wearing cross (4)
7 Stressed-out reindeer herder described by tale (9)
8 Goddess leads a double life? (4)
9 General Custer's last sidelong look (4)
11 Some seafarers in the distance (4)
13 Thick fog, very high (4)
15 Chief shortstop has red gown (9)
16 Places to play games, you may say at first (4)
17 Pinching that woman, father ran (6)

DOWN

2 Just say no to dregs (6)
3 Emblems of family business, collecting grain on granges (5,2,4)
4 Aquatic animal eating plant's first leaf (5)
5 Grace is in Smith's partner's unemployment (11)
6 Can't do without massage, reportedly (4)
10 Go after prize money, taking third place in tournament (6)
12 Quick foray involves chief of police (5)
14 Somersaulting, by the way in the old spot (4)

Answer, page 399

ACROSS

1 Congreve plays have a common focus (8)
7 Waggish nobleman turned left (5)
8 $1,000 invested in unfurnished garbage boat (5)
9 Means to check stories and songs about swinging octet (3,8)
11 Top cop initially tagged one in Italy—Rome, perhaps (7,4)
16 Follow wagon heading west to terminal in Minsk (5)
17 Four going back with something to eat (5)
18 They're recognized in one-horse buggy (8)

DOWN

2 In magical land, I find fresh air (5)
3 First of ladies entering the 5th Avenue gate (5)
4 Hayseed covers loss in foreign currency (5)
5 Wish one hadn't beheaded bird (5)
6 Live audio business sold out (8)
7 Fine time to catch Yale student with bit of cocaine (8)
10 Drink from the jar, oddly (3)
12 Pass every piece of fruit (5)
13 To understand a sign (5)
14 Smart, giving up $100 prize (5)
15 Incredibly angry, I scold (5)

Answer, page 399

ACROSS

1 Weight of horseshoe in water (5)
4 Student's back talk aroused running back (5)
7 Resident of Hollywood is tragic poet (5)
8 No acting president (5)
9 Actor/author taking boy east, then south (5,6)
10 Begin the meeting, using copycat tactics described by binder? (4,2,5)
14 Swordsman's tracks found in wildlife park (5)
15 Clumsy writer backed into it (5)
16 Must have seen about 500 boomerangs (5)
17 Sullen; low-down; ultimately gloomy (5)

DOWN

1 School dance band's advertisement (5)
2 America invaded by north Italian platoons (5)
3 *Entertainment Tonight* in possession of awards: they're a blast (11)
4 Treating pneumonia, M.D. causes panic (11)
5 Detective rejected law for a spot on TV? (5)
6 Nothing coming up on Kansas golf course (5)
10 Deceive one of the family, in a manner of speaking (5)
11 Join Pierre's mother, clutching $1,000 (5)
12 Spanish man to vanish twice? (5)
13 Wretched Republican lawyer (5)

9

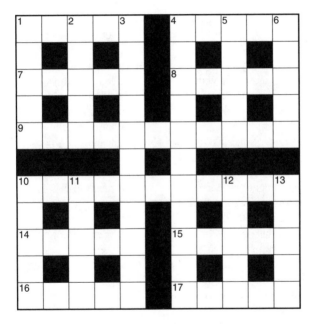

Answer, page 400

ACROSS

1 Develop spare photo as a sign of ownership? (10)

8 Shooter with a gun, empty (5)

9 Lilies from ballooners, not oddly (5)

10 Dessert made with a variety of vitamins? (4)

11 Team turned on inventor (6)

13 Lost soldier taken in by sloth, perhaps, or monkey (6)

15 I caught you concealing piece of information, in a state (4)

18 In different circumstances, it includes f-number (2,3)

19 Show last part of maneuver the wrong way (5)

20 Confounded, slow-talkin' smart alecks (4-2-4)

DOWN

2 Beginning to pull disgusting practical joke (5)

3 Speaks to illiterates about opening of upper Egyptian port (4)

4 Carrying stick, run across African land (6)

5 Sanctimonious person's first debts (5)

6 Where one is in transition, in general (10)

7 Tangle with gal on both sides of street … a real hothead? (10)

12 Say, "Might I drink?" (3,3)

14 It's mixed among fruit (5)

16 Remove top of tool shed (5)

17 Stadium loses north field (4)

Answer, page 400

ACROSS

1 European land is free of any source of illness (4)

4 Tailless monkey eating foremost of meadow grass (6)

7 Gossip with host about continuing conflict (10)

8 Implement for stirring a bit of pancake mix (6)

9 Point of land shown in carbon copy (4)

10 Little woman's husband's first kid (4)

12 Cosmetic product might, if worn by Dee (6)

14 Origin of spirited dance in which baker is involved? (10)

15 Poetry almost understood Texas city (6)

16 True love in back of gold car (4)

DOWN

2 In French, scoffed about beginning of assault attempted in London (11)

3 Thought of doctor accepting application (5)

4 Act includes young male dandy (5)

5 Impersonate La Bohème, approximately (5)

6 Being seen everywhere in Missouri returning gift (11)

11 Cause of itching I have located in high school (5)

12 Animal seen in A&P? Just the opposite (5)

13 Be certain about a candymaker (5)

Answer, page 401

ACROSS

1 Wild mornings with some women (6)

7 Aloof and piscine? (6)

8 On the way back, place fresh rose (4,2)

9 Stop putting antique in box (4,2)

10 Photographers arrived with crude sign (11)

14 Former Asian leader in hot tub, shivering (6)

15 Storm envelops popular valley (6)

16 A supporting beam not on the boat (6)

17 Backer's dashed off line in contract (6)

DOWN

2 Inability to read draft 11A (6)

3 Current quality in play's opening (3,3)

4 Actress's boy stashing small container for liquid rock (6,5)

5 Some Hebrew is dominant knowledge (6)

6 Pale invitation's info includes it (6)

10 They'll slither in firm underwear (6)

11 Rambling leader of minority, openly gay, extremely happy (6)

12 "Twist o' Meat"? (6)

13 Stevenson keeps still (4,2)

Answer, page 401

ACROSS

1 Brief intermission after the opening—Gene takes stretch (4,4)

6 Haley book about Britain's first factory workers? (6)

7 Established face of Liddy Dole (4)

8 I'm about to cover pink slip with long skirt (4)

9 Aides finally make a suggestion without obfuscation (6)

10 Feline eating piece of Central American plant (6)

13 Modernize ruby ring (4)

15 45,600 clothing stands (4)

16 Youngster in Chicago hiding in vase (6)

17 One gets into plating ugly ashtray from trash? (3,5)

DOWN

1 Vain one finally understood revision in italics (11)

2 Debut of *Twenty Questions* assignments (5)

3 "Best in the land" boxer has possibility to get weaker (3-8)

4 Foremost of tailors is going to weave (5)

5 Painter to leave Connecticut school before the second half (4)

11 In trial, I billed defense (5)

12 Occupy illegally, as if residing in street (5)

14 Lawyers adopting one platform (4)

13

Answer, page 402

ACROSS

4 Someone accepting souvenir, returned after inspection (10)

7 Broadcast *Topper*? Who cares? (2,4)

8 Joke with a lunatic (4)

9 Profit's holding ... yes or no (4)

11 Check baseball team's comeback (4)

13 Tiger engages first of horses in conversation (4)

14 Having unpaid checks: unknown amount (6)

16 Cautious when consuming "Summer Wine" (10)

DOWN

1 Waifish models' look, daring to maintain tiny measurement (6,4)

2 Husband's first son coming up to eat (4)

3 Promise trouble (6)

5 Wounds countess, with seconds to go (4)

6 Say I'm invested in part-time hiring of troops (10)

10 Catch parent swimming (6)

12 Try to win someone's heart, diamond, or club (4)

15 Noted diarist on eastern baseball team (4)

14

Answer, page 402

ACROSS

1 Ought to assume as a responsibility without hesitation (6)

5 Before a king, my group appears shaky (4)

7 Associated with Air Force, military group provided backing (10)

8 Evil character rushed to an auditor (4)

9 Sheltered by old stranger, live somewhere in Texas (6)

10 CD boxes fail to be sealed (6)

13 I missed double-zero, by the way (4)

15 Be at workshop, painting fine composer (4,6)

16 Service branch's refusal to accept victory (4)

17 One way to discriminate distorted images (6)

DOWN

2 Impressively large, they changed when fluorinated? (5)

3 Run all over the place … assuming I have to rush out everywhere (11)

4 Doctor not very good in practice (5)

5 Crews are out swimming in river (11)

6 Further notice about Eisenhower (5)

11 Name of a country written the wrong way in *Playbill* (5)

12 Woman's name made from five pieces of bread? (5)

14 Dances for thousands? (5)

15

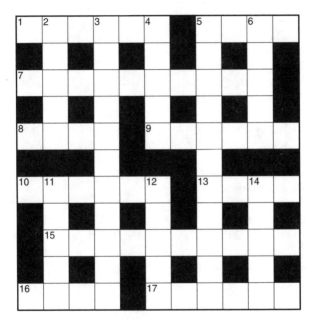

Answer, page 403

ACROSS

1 Eat and run (4)
3 Country singer's opening with "Paradise" (6)
7 Breathe convulsively and quietly after anesthetic (4)
8 Just after false alarm (6)
10 In autumn, there's no place to gamble for sport (8)
13 Top of tree loaded with salt (8)
16 Taking leave, you rejected fairness (6)
17 Male wearing one short garment (4)
18 Missouri River interrupted by the dam (6)
19 Items laid, for example, by thousands (4)

DOWN

1 Leave ... leave in the nude? (3,3)
2 Something you'll learn without working (6)
4 Combat flyer to turn from the straight and narrow course (8)
5 Follows general into turf, heading north (4)
6 Letter other than E (4)
9 A bishop's accepted the liqueur (8)
11 A facial feature ultimately becoming sore (6)
12 Intelligent one misguidedly seeking damages about employee's termination (6)
14 Ms. West's upset with wrinkle (4)
15 Coach finally went bankrupt (4)

16

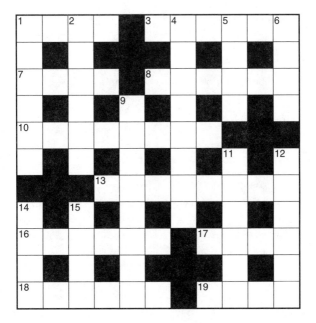

Answer, page 403

ACROSS

1 Fix the program, having understood about Web after the outset (5)
4 Said formalwear in plastic surgeon's work (5)
7 Splendid lawn chore after twisting it off (3,3,1,4)
8 Cowardly cry in pain (6)
9 Head of lettuce in family's oven (4)
11 Unknown man comprehends a socialist writer (4)
12 Specialized talk—initially, just gas (6)
15 Top-notch kite flying disrupted by lousy cast in play (2,3,4,2)
16 Useful hint about mid-July bloom (5)
17 Parcel in church for clergy (5)

DOWN

1 Time to eat very loud duck on TV (5)
2 Global treaty rewritten after general is killed in major skirmish (6,5)
3 Disco lover originally carries bubble in big number (6)
4 Rent rate is changed (4)
5 Pilot's worry: freezing coil must be repaired without fail (7,4)
6 Astronomer put first of names at the bottom of long story (5)
10 Crazed mother raised murderous brother (6)
11 Intended me to meet worker (5)
13 Nick Nolte's face captured initially in hot shot (5)
14 Slow-witted fellow, with stick-pin, dropping in (4)

17

Answer, page 404

ACROSS

4 Verbal changes in store for sportscaster (4,6)

7 Female meadow bug (4)

8 In a high pitch, utter Spanish word for what's found in southern Alaska (6)

9 Lass captivates eastern Highlander (4)

10 Tall pine (4)

13 Partnership requires time with Dorothy's aunt (6)

15 Performs with new cast (4)

16 Among willow spikes, you'll see the swinging guitarist (4,6)

DOWN

1 Pilot through wearing scarf, in the past (6)

2 Guys shelled out for list of options (4)

3 Shattering into smithereens, right? (10)

5 Loyalty, for example, sustained by league (10)

6 Problem with speech is included in record (4)

11 Land of magic refuges in mountains (6)

12 What I have written up about disco song (1.1.1.1.)

14 Mr. Carey had an attraction (4)

18

Answer, page 404

ACROSS

1 Penetrating wind cut ends off rowboat in the Sound (4)

4 Amphetamine after small meal (6)

7 Prepare to fight an independent designer (6)

8 Argue very loudly after *Return of the Creature*? (4)

9 *Green Mile* is terrible (4)

10 Violence could be limiting (6)

11 Help the waiter carrying the woman's plants (6)

14 Frilly skirt that's quite pretentious, you say? (4)

15 Time a gym record (4)

16 Zero profit without powerful combination (3-3)

17 Comment from Seinfeld's neighbor taken the wrong way (6)

18 Say, "A whiskey with a twist?" (4)

DOWN

2 British judge takes unsatisfactory sedative (11)

3 Delete article written in Gaelic (5)

4 "Earthquake in Mexico" (6 March) (5)

5 Brief and meaningful poem's beginning with one of you (5)

6 Iron structure in excellent condition; soft fabric wore out (6,5)

12 Laugh about desire for howling animal (5)

13 Agitated in South Bend? (5)

14 Letter from the Transit Authority (5)

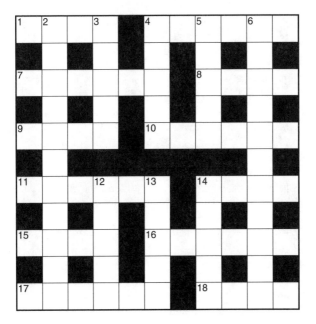

19

Answer, page 405

ACROSS

1 Stealing outside of hospital involved in cuts? (8)

6 Friend of McBeal on TV (4)

7 Minute antenna receiving agent's last stuff (8)

9 Try to mislead first of ladies in the nude (5)

12 Feature of cabin: free backing or loft, perhaps (4,5)

13 Time to relocate in betraying Duke (9)

15 Japanese descendants in retreat—that is wrong (5)

17 Party companion gets in control (8)

18 Groom's response, pursuing female dog (4)

19 Most apt to find fault with last of linemen and Texas A&M tackle (8)

DOWN

1 Jokester in Colorado, at the Center (8)

2 Shouts, "Of course it moved around" (8)

3 Case of papers for pilot, flying solo at last (9)

4 California winery not completing about 3.8 gallons (5)

5 Staff leader nearly cut off? (4)

8 Rich pair of abbots undoing nuts (9)

10 Sure to lose 25%, baron is solvent (8)

11 Least distinct note in trial (8)

14 Deceived five finalists in British tennis tournament (3,2)

16 One knight raised flower (4)

20

Answer, page 405

Rhyming Picture Puzzles

Steve Ryan

• • • • • • • • • • • • • •

Hints on page 382
Answers on page 406

INTRODUCTION

. . . .

I'm sure you've heard the phrase "a picture is worth a thousand words." Well, that's not the case here. Each rhyming picture puzzle in this book is worth only two words. That's because each puzzle illustrates a *super-duper* two-word *rhyme time* experience that's silly to say and lots of fun to play. For example: If you were to see a puzzle showing Mickey Mouse's girlfriend after she went on a crash diet and lost a few too many pounds, the answer would be *Skinny Minnie*.

Each picture has two ways to play. First, try to solve a picture puzzle just as you see it on the page. If it's a *no go* and the solution eludes you, don't worry. The second level of play gives you a *new clue*. The initial letters to the two words in the rhyme (which always have the same number of syllables) can be found on page 382. And, if by chance you get completely stumped, all the answers can be found on page 406.

Some puzzles are pushovers, others are real head-bangers. Some are designed to tickle your funny bone, while others are there to challenge the outer limits of your imagination. But they're all fair and designed to make puzzlers of all ages smile awhile.

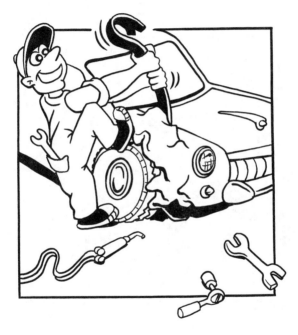

Crypto-Quotes

Leslie Billig

Hints on pages 383–384
Answers on pages 407–419

INTRODUCTION
••••••••••••••••••••••
With Hints for Solving Crypto-Quotes

Crypto-quotes are quotations in a simple substitution code. Each letter of the quotation has been replaced by another letter. A letter is always represented by the same letter throughout the code. For example:

C O D E D   S E N T E N C E S
X L P I P   Y I H M I H X I Y

In this code, the C's are represented by X's, the O by L, the D's by P's, etc. The code will be consistent throughout the puzzle, but a different code is used for each puzzle. A letter will never stand for itself.

There are a number of things to look for that will help you crack the code. Here are some hints:

A one-letter word is always A or I. In a two-letter word, one letter must be a vowel.

A word with an apostrophe before the last letter is going to end in N'T (as in CAN'T), 'S (IT'S), 'M (I'M), or 'D (HE'D). Two letters after an apostrophe might be 'LL (WE'LL), 'VE (I'VE), or 'RE (THEY'RE).

Certain common words have distinct letter patterns. For example: DID, THAT, NEVER, LITTLE, and PEOPLE.

Some words occur over and over simply because they're so commonly written and spoken. Keep an eye out for THE, AND, NOT, YOU, and WITH, for example. In addition, look out for words ending in -ED, -ING, -LESS, -NESS, and -TION.

In these puzzles, which get harder as you go, the quotation is followed by the name of the person who said or wrote it. Often the person's name can be figured out, which will give you more letters with which to decode the quotation.

If you get stuck, there is a solving hint for each crypto-quote on pages 383–384, which will tell you what letter one of the code letters stands for. If you're still stumped, move on to another crypto-quote and then go back to the problematic one later. Sometimes all you need is to look at it with fresh eyes. Remember,

D C   L X   C D U J X   B P G   Z P K ' X

J G I I H H Z ,   X U B ,   X U B   L Y L D K .*

For me, the best thing about writing this book was rediscovering that crypto-quotes are *fun*—fun to decode, and fun to uncover the nuggets of wit and wisdom and who said them. I hope you agree.

*Answer to this cryptogram is on page 407.

1 QFL HCVPS PX V
ANSWLCEZK NCJVS; PQ
XQVCQX QFL BPSZQL RNZ
JLQ ZT PS QFL BNCSPSJ
VSW WNLX SNQ XQNT
ZSQPK RNZ JLQ QN QFL
NEEPGL. —CNHLCQ ECNXQ

2 COXBX TBX CVK CDGXR
DI T GTI'R ADHX VOXI OX
ROKQAU IKC RNXPQATCX:
VOXI OX PTI'C THHKBU DC,
TIU VOXI OX PTI.

        —GTBY CVTDI

3 MFX BH BC MFOK MO

CZVL CA SAY, MO'PO HZBY

CA GO DPZXBKS, GIC MFOK

SAY CZVLH CA IH, MO'PO

HUFBWADFPOKBU?

      — VBVX CAEVBK

4 LCY UWYTL LCGKU TASBL

LCY NSIGYE GE MSB'WY

UGIGKU XYSXVY VGLLVY

LGKM XGYQYE SO LGNY

LCTL LCYM KYIYW OSWUYL.

      —ZGNNM ELYPTWL

5 JTJQCEGJQJ X AL X'B
ORNJU XW X SGXZN SGJ
YZXTJQRXSC RSXWFJR
EQXSJQR. BC LMXZXLZ XR
SGOS SGJC ULZ'S RSXWFJ
JZLYAG LW SGJB.

— WFOZZJQC L'KLZZLQ

6 AN CBCR'Z LMM KVSN
VUND VR ZXN PLSN PXBQ,
YHZ AN'DN LMM BR ZXN
PLSN YVLZ.

— YNDRLDC YLDHKX

138

7 ZW WPPE QS OSBSJWSSJ
ISGKO WP ASW WFKSS
WFPTOGJC FZWO ZJ
LGOSLGDD. Z CZC ZW ZJ
PJS GRWSKJPPJ PJ WFS
APDR UPTKOS.

      — FGJE GGKPJ

8 MWUCU'A TB MCRJD MB
IURTN F WPZBCRAM GWUT
XBP WFKU MWU GWBHU
NBKUCTZUTM GBCDRTN EBC
XBP.   — GRHH CBNUCA

9 L ENXVZ POMV UEZQ
BEZMVHGOXLEZG ALXP
RTGVUN, OZJ L OR GE
BUVMVH XPOX GERVXLRVG
L JEZ'X YZJVHGXOZJ O
GLZQUV AEHJ L OR
GOTLZQ.   —EGBOH ALUJV

10 MIKXCJ KCC WIM OKM
ZLKMA KAUIXZNLJ, SDL NR
JGD BKML LG LIZL K WKM'Z
OTKXKOLIX, PNUI TNW
VGBIX.

        —KSXKTKW CNMOGCM

11 WLCHOBCHW BO'W
MHPHWWSQJ OL FL S ALMF
ZBWOSMPH LKO LU ODH
VSJ BM LQZHQ OL PLCH
NSPX S WDLQO ZBWOSMPH
PLQQHPOAJ.

— HZVSQZ SANHH

12 ZP YZP V EYX XY XOYIVT
PJCTYB. CA CX ZPMPB'X
AYM OCI, ZP'J RP
ZVXUOCBH XPEPNCTCYB RF
UVBJEPECHOX.

— ICEYB RPMEP

13 SMLMK PMTT GMUGTM
FUV PU XU PFBSEY. PMTT
PFMC VFOP PU XU OSX
PFMH VBTT YDKGKBYM HUD
VBPF PFMBK BSEMSDBPH.
　　　　　　　—EMUKEM GOPPUS

14 UDD BVFR QYDQSY
YHQYPU CDFWYZK AZDB
WYBDPZVPR, CTYF UTY
BDKU CDFWYZAXS UTGFJ
DA VSS GK NXKU TVOGFJ
GU.　　　—CVSUYZ CGFPTYSS

15 P MKZKAVUJI UY
YHLKHQK CSH CHVRY
SPVF PZZ SUY ZUWK JH
AKMHLK CKZZ-RQHCQ,
PQF JSKQ CKPVY FPVR
DZPYYKY JH PBHUF AKUQD
VKMHDQUEKF.

— WVKF PZZKQ

16 BOT AGP BU FGBFO G
WRCFWSTHGSS KN BU AGKB
CRBKS BOT HGSS NBUEN
MUSSKRD GRJ BOTR EKFW
KB CE. — HUH CTFWTM

17 ADQNQ INQ AMF TPJEBAJ
PF DEVIP GQTPU MTBB
QPSENQ: ADIA DQ DIJ PF
JQPJQ FX DEVFN, IPS ADIA
DQ DIJ PQHQN OPFMP
ANFEGBQ.

— JTPLBITN BQMTJ

18 KBT UBI IB WM LVQMXTY
NX KBT ABH'I CHBG
GRMQM KBT'QM UBNHU,
WMLVTFM KBT SNURI HBI
UMI IRMQM.

— KBUN WMQQV

19 OD DMMX ET QOQDTTV
FTKAY DM ZOYPMGTA O
RKZ VM DKBTVD QMA
SAODOVL, UWD O
PMWBZV'D LOGT OD WN
UTPKWYT UF DRKD DOET O
SKY DMM QKEMWY.

      — AMUTAD UTVPRBTF

20 ZLN IDZ WV
QGTDSSLGACVQ GJ ZLN
JDGE, WNC ZLN DPV
QLLIVQ GJ ZLN QLA'C CPZ.

      — WVYVPEZ TGEET

21 VWG SPQJ VWKPZ K
EGZEGV YNSMV IJ CYTV KT
VWG QGPZVW SH KV. KH K
WYU VS QKFG IJ QKHG
YZYKP, K'U IYOG VWG
TYIG IKTVYOGT, SPQJ
TSSPGE.

   — VYQQMQYW NYPOWGYU

22 X QSXOJSXO JBSJ JBP
ZBCSVP "S FKON ZKPQ" XV
VXQZFI S HKOJCSGXHJXKO
XO JPCQV.

      — PGNSC SFFSO ZKP

23 CKMCQK QKXEU
PMNKRVAUH KFKES TXS,
XUT X QMR MB RANKP AR'P
RVXR DVXR RVKS QKXEUKT
RVK TXS JKBMEK DXP
DEMUH.   —JAQQ FXLHVXU

24 DJ'BJ AWX LONUVKJ-
XIDP JUIPIQNUF NP LAJ
UIGPLOH ZIO HJWOF PID,
WPX QIFL IZ GF WOJP'L
JBJP XWQC HJL.
                —QIKKH NBNPF

25 AV KVS SCI PVFS
PVUDKY PVPIKSF VM VTG
BDUIF MDKA TF JBB
RDSCVTS RVGAF?

    — PJGZIB PJGZIJT

26 LQRRNI MBI QE DOI
MGSGMCR HICQKR GOIZ
XMDOIC DQLI EDMCDE
TMDTOQZB VH GQDO
LKDOIC ZMDVCI.

    — OMCKNR TKXXQZ

27 KCIISAK YSDNFBCY MXGI

TCBQXGC ENX YNA'I RNDC

Q LQA SG QRLNGI QG

GSRRE QG KCIISAK LQFFSCY

MXGI TCBQXGC ENX YN.

— UGQ UGQ KQTNF

28 ILJLD YLIB ZEETR, NED

IE EIL LJLD DLPXDIR PGLA;

PGL EIYM ZEETR F GVJL FI

AM YFZDVDM VDL ZEETR

PGVP EPGLD NEYT GVJL

YLIP AL. — VIVPEYL NDVIKL

29 EJS EWFAHRS VQEJ

SPANRQEG QD EJNE VS

FORG TSDQWS QE VQEJ

FAW DABSWQFWD.

—JSOWG HSKPAS

30 O WEC'U UQOCJ EK XHH

UQL ZORLAS DPU EK XHH

UQL DLXPUS UQXU RUOHH

ALZXOCR.　　　—XCCL KAXCJ

31 EDKXK FXK EMY EDHROI
EDFE MHTT VK VKTHKZKC
YL FRU SFR MDFEIYKZKX,
FRC YRK YL EDKS HI EDFE
DK DFI EFJKR EY CXHRJ.

— VYYED EFXJHROEYR

32 Q HDMDPQUJQT JR
RWFDYWKX NBW NWT'P
DQP QTXPBJTM PBQP ZQT
BQHD ZBJEKUDT.

— KQHJK YUDTTDU

33 X H S B V G D N F C V
D N Y C R N L C V G K , V R R P C
C G K H Y N R , I G H O L H Q C
V Z H S R H R P C Q J C H J D C R P V G
X H S I G H O V Z H S R
X H S Q W C D Y .

      — Z C Q X D L V Q I P V L

34 G C H N T K D V T F Q N S D J G D
M T W R E S D N J C S D Q M T
D N S J G J G N J N W W M U J G D V S
E G V W O S D T J M E M H D K N E P
G M H D .   — K V W W E M Q K R

35 W VJMJU RQIYX
IVXJUTOBVX GQA OAQ FJV
RBV AUWOJ B SQQL
OQEJOGJU; OQ FJ OGBO'T
YWLJ OGUJJ ZJQZYJ
EJOOWVE OQEJOGJU OQ
GBMJ B SBSD.

—JMJYDV ABIEG

36 BRK BDSFVMK YCBR
MCPK CI BRK PJAB MJIK CA
BRJB XSF OKB BS BRK
SBRKD KIN CI JI JYPFM
RFDDX.　　—USRI UKIAKI

37 VDU ZVUCD'Q ZHCKVBUY
DUG MEDZC GHQFVTQ
KVDCUDQHDX QV MVCU
CHXFQ VJ QFU CFVYU JVY
E BUYA MVDX QHSU.

— EDZYU XHZU

38 T RLBXD VP QMVHVIEMR
BRBTKKD NQFQTKR LGTL
LGQ AQRL LEIQ LV ABD
THDLGEHY ER KTRL DQTN.

— ITNLD TKKQH

39 CXZ'W CQZY WJGIJDLIY

JB X ZIH QYIX ZIKIG UBIW

PXDT JB QJW BGQUQZXE

YQCIZWQBZW.

   — BEQKIG HIZYIEE LBECIW

40 OQ CGW TFDYOV YOPWR

ISF, ISF'BW LSSH.

RGZPWRTWZBW AZR Z

VSKKSM, HSAM-CS-WZBCG

ABOCWB OM GOR HZI.

        — KOVPWI RTOYYZMW

41 KXEY XF YIFXYU MJIP

THB'Q MJXPS; IKK MJIM XF

PYZYFFIUT XF MH IZZYGM

MJY XAGHFFXDKY, QH

CXMJHBM MJY

XPQXFGYPFIDKY, IPQ DYIU

MJY XPMHKYUIDKY.

   — SIMJKYYP PHUUXF

42 O YG PBMV Y FJUMOZ

KBAKNAYOBKN RQP QYW

JBCKNWAPPC QOW AOGK.

   — FYUMP FOZYWWP

43 ZFKLLKX ML CWK EQT
JWR, WQUMTY TRCWMTY CR
LQD, QZLCQMTL AGRE
YMUMTY JRGXD KUMXKTOK
RA CWK AQOC.

— YKRGYK KFMRC

44 OZHUFUWD UD RZF S ISE
OLZMJDDUZR. UM XZP
DPWWJJE FKJLJ SLJ TSRX
LJVSLED, UM XZP
EUDNLSWJ XZPLDJHM XZP
WSR SHVSXD VLUFJ S IZZG.

— LZRSHE LJSNSR

45 CNU YZAGC ZV SAJAGF,
QGW ZV IUAGF QG
ZYCAPAEC, AE CZ IU
VZZSAEN UGZDFN CZ
IUSAUJU CNU IUEC AE BUC
CZ HZPU. —YUCUL DECAGZJ

46 BKSMSBUTM LOYINW
WIRQIC, LOU YU BSX LT
URMX NRQX QYUK
YXBMTNYLIT WQYHUXTWW.
　　　　—HSYUK LSINQYX

47 ZHSZTAZDPZ AU DMJ

OQKJ QKSSZDU JM VMF; AJ

AU OQKJ VMF WM OAJQ

OQKJ QKSSZDU JM VMF.

— KEWMFU QFHEZV

48 FTN NSDYNDF USG FH

IHWLYWIN ZG JYXD FTSF

FTNG XHW'F QNSPPG WNNX

DHZNFTYWE YD FH ENF YF

OHQ FTNZ.

— MHSW IHPPYWD

49 NII R QWWO AK JNHW N
PKJWOU RM N DNZH, N
DKIRPWJNQ, NQO N
DZWAAU SRZI.

       — PYNZIRW PYNDIRQ

50 S ASY EZDWYO INPPWYD
MWO GWOBUA PZZPM PMZ
CWQOP PWAZ MZ EWPZO
UCC AUQZ PMSY MZ ISY
IMZG.   — MZQE ISZY

51 AZCINEWQQH, L XBLEO
LJ W UNVWE BWIE'X VZX
XBZ CLYBX VWE GH XBZ
XLVZ IBZ'I XUZEXH-JNRC,
IBZ VWH GZ QRPOH.

      — SZGNCWB OZCC

52 P LJQH DR ARKY PE N
BPKQ ZIHKNED BNMDRKI.
IRL MRLFHE'D XNKY
NEIAZQKQ EQNK DZQ
XFNMQ. — JDQCQE AKPWZD

53 QENUN YUN QIK IYCZ KD

ZGUNYBTSF OTFEQ: QK VN

QEN PYSBON KU QEN

WTUUKU QEYQ UNDONPQZ

TQ.   —NBTQE IEYUQKS

54 C QXZI HJ JXKIXOI YLX

UIZJHJMJ HO LXDGHOR LHJ

XYO PHIYJ CTMIZ YI LCPI

IODHRLMIOIG LHK YHML

XWZJ.   —KCDFXDK TXZQIJ

55 PML POCIAKL RBPM PML

QOCHBP DJDPLX MYD

YKRYJD ALLG PMYP BP BD

MBFMKJ IGQOCHBPYAKL PC

XCDP QLCQKL.

                 —L.A. RMBPL

56 SYM SD ROM SNAMGR

OJZLY YMMAG KG OLPKYF

GSZMSYM RS ISYAMW

IOMWM HSJ LWM IOMY HSJ

ASY'R ESZM OSZM LR

YKFOR. —ZLWFLWMR ZMLA

57 DEJ ZOWA DEQOV DEUD
GUYJG HG SKZF DEJ
PHKJUHMKUMA QG QDG
QOJSSQMQJOMA.

       —JHVJOJ FMMUKDEA

58 UZ TDNXQH LOQR NJ
ODZ NXDN WN YDO YWIAQR
NJ FJ TWOXWMF JM
OLMRDZ. ELN XQ MQBQH
ODWR DMZNXWMF DEJLN
RHDY SJAQH.

       —FHJBQH IPQBQPDMR

59 HDI BZM QIXVF Z
CTLDMN RXCT QZHDMNCU,
QIC HDI BZM'C UXC DM XC
JDL VDME.

— QDLXU HNVCUXM

60 BKOC PKKTB ZMC JK PC
JZBJCX, KJGCMB JK PC
BIZYYKICX, ZLX BKOC NCI
JK PC HGCICX ZLX
XAQCBJCX.

— NMZLHAB PZHKL

61 N R Q D U H T M Y A M L U S
F X B K I Q D U T X M L K I
Q D R K B O D H X R H Y D C
N D M N K D C B K K Y B U I H X D B Q
F X B K I Q D U R T D U F X R U H B U S
R T H X D A I M.

       — V R Q V R Q R C R K H D Q T

62 O F M D G M T M I G W S D J M
S M U Y E M G D I V B D C S; E G
E W H I C Z G F E K C M W G Q D G
E F F E G D G M S Z I M F T M W.

       — U Y M M I T E B G H F E D

63 DV ODZ WRPPZS JZTFKYV
ZSDVTM UVMSTZIM SDV
ATKUFV ZYVT ODKWD DV
DKHMVXJ HEMS BRMM.
　　　　　—FVZTFV DVTAVTS

64 NAQ DMH BE ABCH
HYHWGLUBIM HAEH. LN
SDCH D EZVVHEE NJ BL,
GNZ'YH MNL LN ELDWL
GNZIM. 　—JWHQ DELDBWH

65 QYQRHZ YFH YEXYDZ
VBFH NFBPQEH NKYO DBP
NKBPUKN—YOS VBFH
XBOSHFJPE.

—LKYFEHZ BZUBBS

66 XLI JB RM XLI CJCIO
DJRB "GRU DJKI. KJDX
FIIT." FLP JBYIOXRDI? R
JKOIJBP VRDDIB RX.
XLIP'OI EHDX OHGGRMU RX
RM. —PJTZY DVROMZAA

67 HP RUMT YHPFUAP
TISHKR PFIP SUA TFUACE
KMNMD FINM QUDM
OFHCEDMK PFIK SUA FINM
OID YHKEUYT.

— MDQI LUQLMOX

68 HAUHTA SKU SUWO
IVEEVRQ XUSR QAE HJVX
DUWA EKJR HAUHTA SKU
SUWO IEJRXVRQ YH.

— UQXAR RJIK

69 JA TPMX TPD LTZMS
QUKD NVT MJKDE: NQD
AJOEN JP VQJLQ NT HUID
TPD'E HJENUIDE, UPS NQD
EDLTPS JP VQJLQ NT
WOTAJN YX NQDH.

—S.Q. MUVODPLD

70 CVHK NHJNOH RHHN
ZHOODKF EJW ZVYZ EJW
IYK'Z QJ Y ZVDKF, EJW
RDKQ JB ODRH ZJ ZAE DZ.

—LYAFYAHZ IVYGH GLDZV

71 M K D S L Q T F X Q   K V V U K C D

F X   A U   P L Y Y U R   M L F S   F M X

O L Q R D   X P   V X Y L F L E L K Q D —

F S X D U   F C G L Q T   F X   T U F   K Q

L Q Z U D F L T K F L X Q   D F K C F U R ,

K Q R   F S X D U   F C G L Q T   F X   T U F

X Q U   D F X V V U R .

             — U K C Y   M L Y D X Q

72 A D Z ' F   U H   M C V U B H .

Q D C ' T H   Z D F   F M J F   I T H J F .

             — I D B A J   V H S T

73 AGR UKORMNDCYZ GYCL
DW BDIRMCKRCA HYC
CRIRM MROZYHR AGR
GRZOUCB GYCL DW Y
CRUBGTDM.

— GSTRMA G. GSKOGMRP

74 FJBIWKG AC T CAGSG
FRJBIMR ERAQR EG CAXF
BIJ TQLITAPFTPQGC. FRBCG
FBB WAM FB ZTCC FRJBIMR
TJG BIJ XJAGPHC.

— TJKGPG XJTPQAC

75 JQVE UVFF YDBCVX JQD

FCXW NH JQD HYDD NXFZ

EN FNXO CE VJ VE JQD

QNBD NH JQD PYCLD.

           —DFBDY WCLVE

76 MJ ZAX EYL QIID ZAXU

PIYC NPIL YVV YTAXH ZAX

YUI VAOMLF HPIMUO, MH'O

BXOH DAOOMTVI ZAX

PYKIL'H FUYODIC HPI

OMHXYHMAL. —BIYL QIUU

77 UYO HODXHQXNPO UYSJV
XNFKU GYXQOGBOXHO SG
UYXU YO HOXPPR SG TOHR
VFFZ, SJ GBSUO FI XPP
UYO BOFBPO EYF GXR YO
SG TOHR VFFZ.

— HFNOHU VHXTOG

78 M UMK'H DRO OR OMPL
M IRO RY SQKZHGULKO OR
BJZOL M JLMIIC YQKKC
XRRP.

— LJKLHO GLUZKDBMC

79 TES VLJ RLDFNT HSQWR

UBR VBLALVURA EG L XLJ

MT BEY BR UARLUD UBEDR

YBE VLJ QE JEUBFJW GEA

BFX. —HLXRD Q. XFNRD

80 Z VJMO MOQOEZHZGD. Z

VJMO ZM JH LNIV JH

TOJDNMH. FNM Z IJD'M

HMGT OJMZDX TOJDNMH.

—GAHGD YOQQOH

81 PVQ TQDP CFE XADP

TQCJPBYJS PVBFLD BF PVQ

RAZSE UCFFAP TQ DQQF AZ

QWQF PAJUVQE. PVQH XJDP

TQ YQSP RBPV PVQ VQCZP.

         — VQSQF GQSSQZ

82 NWG RO AXEAIMISKI OE

FBJW FEXQ OBJJQOOTBV

NWQS RD ODRXO BA

WIDXQK DWIS NWQS RD

DXRQO DE ODRX BA

TXRQSKVG TQQVRSM?

         — PQXDXISK XBOOQVV

Crosswords

Trip Payne

Answers on pages 420–429

ACROSS

1 Classic soprano role
5 Mission of 1836
10 Earring shape
11 *Pole to Pole* host
12 Word on a coffeehouse menu
13 Wimbledon runner-up's memento
14 Rustic retreat, perhaps
15 Papers used for pads?
16 "So?"
18 Call-in show setting, often
22 Met cries
25 1970s acronym
26 Arrest
27 Greek characters
28 Used interrogation
29 One way to learn
30 Kid
31 Reagan and Wyman, e.g.

DOWN

1 Bon mot, often
2 Shiraz citizen
3 "Nothing ___!"
4 Likely
5 Makes the scene
6 Refrain sounds
7 "Sad to say ..."
8 It's almost valueless
9 Washington settings
15 French paper
17 *The Deptford Trilogy* author
19 Betty Ford offering
20 More than cross
21 Havens
22 Jackanapes
23 It's a trick
24 He wrote the song "My Way"
27 Poetic palindrome

1

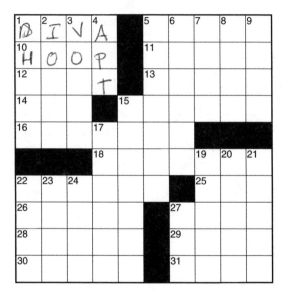

Answer, page 420

ACROSS

1 Broccoli ___
5 Overly virile
10 Sampras, at times
11 Indo-European, once
12 Young follower
13 Jet kin
14 *Corrida* opponent
15 Welsh rarebit ingredient
16 Imitated Izaak Walton
18 Food label abbr.
21 Word with food or water
22 Instances of recidivism
24 The Sugarhill Gang's genre
26 Makes like
27 Big name at the 1976 Olympics
29 Where a necklace clasp lies
30 Shangri-las
31 Bakery assistant
32 Role for Jay Silverheels
33 Minimal change

DOWN

1 Many Jamaicans
2 Prologue follower
3 Oktoberfest establishment
4 Barbara's *Cry Wolf* costar
5 Site of an A.D. 73 siege
6 Shrinking sea
7 The on-line world
8 Prince of the stage
9 Half and half?
17 It's near Juárez
19 Make the hole bigger
20 Set forth
23 Hysterical person
25 Common solecism
27 Take home
28 Bother

2

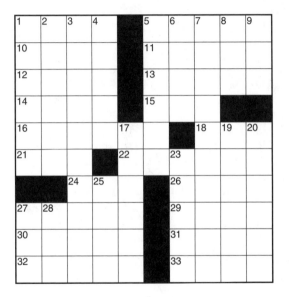

Answer, page 420

ACROSS

1 Pots for pot stickers
5 Members of the Rurik family
10 From scratch
11 Noted book-club leader
12 *Intersection* star
13 The pits
14 Actress Siddons
16 Kate's *Titanic* role
17 Came to the point?
19 Fails
22 Famous fictional estate
23 Word in "Oh Susanna"
27 African antelope
29 Gather
30 Ray of a sort
31 Word on a clapboard
32 Like Heidi
33 Tore

DOWN

1 Wits
2 Draftable
3 Either star of *Tea and Sympathy*
4 Exercise wear, sometimes
5 Heavy weight
6 Leftovers, in a way
7 Spirit
8 Union demand
9 Bit
15 Outwits
18 Andy Capp haunt
19 Checks
20 Series featuring the firm McKenzie, Brackman
21 Rafsanjani, for one
24 Tide table term
25 Hunky-dory
26 Newspaper page
28 Article written by Einstein

Answer, page 421

ACROSS

1 They're coming out
5 Actuate
10 Prepare for printing
11 Group numbering about 340,000
12 Mendacious person
13 Free sample, e.g.
14 Bind
16 Movie shot
17 "Beg pardon?"
19 Sorghum product
23 *Arabian Nights* subject
26 Leon Uris book
27 "Bis!"
29 Best Picture nominee of 1995
30 Origami creation, often
31 Skater Heiden
32 *South Park* character
33 *The Canterbury Tales* characters' destination

DOWN

1 Removes, in a way
2 Minneapolis suburb
3 Kind of roll
4 They're often drawn
5 Publicly accuse
6 Dent, perhaps
7 Low-down
8 *Cope Book* name
9 Great Britain emblem
15 Curry accompaniment, at times
18 He has the question for every answer
20 Where millions of connections are made every year
21 Notable vaccine developer
22 Dismiss
23 Prepare for a break
24 Fiend
25 *Funny Lady* actor
28 Bed-and-breakfast, often

4

1	2	3	4		5	6	7	8	9
10					11				
12					13				
14				15			16		
17						18			
			19				20	21	22
23	24	25		26					
27			28			29			
30						31			
32						33			

Answer, page 421

ACROSS

1 Monte Solaro's setting
6 Throng
10 *Manhattan* director
11 Appear
12 Novel featuring the lawsuit *Jarndyce v. Jarndyce*
14 Comic partner of 7-Down
15 Appetite
16 It's on the side
18 *Salamandridae* members
22 Judges
24 Seal
25 Jr.'s son, often
27 "___ Fool to Care" (1954 hit)
28 He sold over 300 million records
32 Finis
33 Bracelet setting
34 Hacker's term
35 Meddled

DOWN

1 Went by brougham
2 Touch upon, with "to"
3 Rush undergoer
4 Best Actor nominee of 1992
5 Black
6 Tea accompaniments
7 Comic partner of 14-Across
8 Dash lengths
9 Almost invisible
13 Female Wyandotte
17 Border crosser, sometimes
19 Kitchen utensils
20 Spill
21 Held on
23 Editor's insertion
26 Turkmenistan neighbor
28 Short do
29 Plant that was sacred to Bacchus
30 It's far from gross
31 *Starpeace* recorder

5

Answer, page 422

ACROSS

1 Carriage of a sort
5 Iceberg location
10 Start over
11 Thunderstruck
12 Novel about a whale ship mutiny
13 Startled reaction
14 Rafter inhabitant, sometimes
16 Supplement, with "out"
17 Luther listing
21 Under control
23 It does a bang-up job
24 Vivaciously
26 Dull
29 Put on the line
30 Disco singer Ward
31 Like some threats
32 Sign on a door
33 Georgia has two of them

DOWN

1 NASA fact-gatherers
2 *Always*, e.g.
3 Went heavy on the relish?
4 Outhouse symbol
5 Bartender's remark
6 Active
7 You can't stand having one
8 George of the Jungle's pal
9 Start of an Iowa city
15 Living room piece
18 It's a big step
19 Isolate
20 Stirs up
22 Sharp
25 Guardhouse
26 Head left
27 *Approximately Infinite Universe* artist
28 Former presidential pet

6

Answer, page 422

ACROSS

1 Its first president was Ngarta Tombalbaye
5 Make healthier, in a way
10 Kent colleague
11 Gainesville neighbor
12 The O of REO Speedwagon
13 Sunday supplement, in slang
14 Person with seniority
16 Word with pack or pick
17 Pin seeker
20 Rink need, once
22 Edwin Starr hit
23 Many of these could make a lot
26 Gray
29 Mouse pad?
30 It's a snap
31 Profile feature
32 What you might get at a bar before your meal
33 Arab League member

DOWN

1 Blockhead
2 Head light?
3 "Factory" worker
4 Kyzyl Kum, for one
5 Happy friend
6 *A Theory of Semiotics* author
7 TV setting, often
8 Kiddie-lit heroine
9 Duty imposer
15 Genealogist's word
18 Uptempo music genre
19 Uptempo music genre
20 Bandies
21 Buckwheat product
24 Actress Martinelli
25 Taken in
27 Symbol of viscosity
28 It was east of Eden

7

Answer, page 423

ACROSS

1 Orchestra leader Baxter
4 "Go on ..."
10 Former Miss America host
11 Swamp honeysuckle, e.g.
12 Word in a Tennessee Williams title
13 Home-ec activity
14 Cries of discovery
16 Staff members
17 Pests
19 Penitent words
23 Retrogresses
26 Tide type
27 Quad location
29 Stray
30 What A can stand for
31 Center of gravity?
32 Student, at times
33 Hosp. areas

DOWN

1 Admit
2 Root of government
3 Church meeting
4 Smidgen
5 Where the Boston Mountains are
6 Assumes
7 "Y" wearers
8 Spring period
9 Hangs back
15 Small piece
18 Cynical response
20 *Deathtrap* star
21 Less well-done
22 Site of three World War I battles
23 Get going
24 Kind of duck
25 Devilkins
28 Date

8

Answer, page 423

ACROSS

1 Take a trip
5 Opposite of up
10 Recitative follower
11 *Twin Peaks* character
12 "___ Help" (#1 hit from 1974)
13 Put away
14 "Tea for Two" singer
16 Worthless
17 Interdict
20 Three short, three long, three short
21 Mrs. Robinson's daughter
23 Average guy
24 Orange or peach
27 Harassed
28 Arrack flavoring
29 Dismisses
30 Browser requirement
31 Do a greenhouse task

DOWN

1 Hits the ground, perhaps
2 Citation commander
3 Tropical climbers
4 Keglers' places
5 Hip
6 E or G, e.g.
7 Monokini lack
8 The middle of summer?
9 Morse T
15 Prove it!
17 Keesler Air Force Base location
18 Cell ends
19 Most unfamiliar
22 Presidential middle name
23 Muralist Orozco
24 Machine piece
25 One of *Two Virgins*
26 Stopper

Answer, page 424

ACROSS

1 Sketch (out)
4 Dishevel
10 Opening number?
11 Cast
12 Park, often
14 Marvin K. Mooney's chronicler
15 Flabbergast
16 Characters in *The Odyssey*?
18 Hosp. settings
19 Adverse
22 To be, in Barcelona
24 Boating hazard
26 Chilling
30 Bush setting, once
32 Sherpa, usually
33 100 centavos
34 Foreigner, for example
35 USN rank

DOWN

1 Bryophytic organism
2 Hand's cost
3 Cole Porter's birthplace
4 Doctor's paper
5 Excuse
6 Samovars
7 It's mined in Maine
8 Aye-aye's kin
9 Perfect spots
13 Clairvoyance
17 Think best
19 Oscar winner of 1990
20 Bank
21 Sudden transitions
23 Yellow card issuer
25 Insipid
27 Be on the up-and-up?
28 Desktop picture
29 Sargasso Sea denizens
31 Root word?

Answer, page 424

ACROSS

1 Inform (on)
4 Having raised areas
10 Princetonian's rival
11 Think
12 Coaster of a sort
14 Picard's command
15 *Night Court* actor
16 Contacts' alternatives
21 Cynic's expression
23 Singer Dando
24 It starts near Peru
26 Consultant, often
30 Kind of run
31 It's past *due*
32 Sex cell
33 Drafting board: Abbr.

DOWN

1 Changes the length of, in a way
2 Certain support group
3 Feel pins and needles
4 1994 Tony-winning actress
5 Chills out
6 Half of a prayer
7 Perambulate
8 *Printemps* follower
9 "___ Bingle" (Crosby's nickname)
13 Dorothy's last name in *The Wizard of Oz*
17 *Bonnie and Clyde* director
18 Runs out
19 Chairmakers, sometimes
20 Sleeps soundly?
22 Find new tenants
25 Work as a stevedore
26 It's commonly felt
27 Man of the arts
28 It's a bit of work
29 *Discreet Music* recorder

11

Answer, page 425

ACROSS

1 He performs with Lucille
7 May celebrant
10 Sister of Polyhymnia
11 *Fables in Slang* author
12 Cried out
13 *Winter of Artifice* novelist
14 Balloon
15 Weight
16 Nat "King" Cole's birthplace
18 State follower, often
21 Symbol of a Moslem who's returned from a Mecca pilgrimage
22 Teed off
26 Comparison of easiness
27 Eisenhower appointee
28 One way to stand
29 Most unapproachable
30 Show stoppers
31 Mean

DOWN

1 Believes
2 Concoct
3 Mustard relative
4 Properly situated
5 Metal ornamentation
6 One of Israel's twelve tribes
7 Unexpected assistance, symbolically
8 Antipathy
9 High-IQ society
15 Ohio institution
17 Cite
18 *Ship Arriving Too Late to Save a Drowning Witch* musician
19 24-book work
20 Meter readers?
23 It comes in a tub
24 Endow
25 Ferrara family name
27 Finished

12

Answer, page 425

ACROSS

1 Lute feature
5 Opposite of 26-Across
10 Pan alternative
11 Daily Double variety
12 Usual way to sleep
13 Vegas temptations
14 Wrap that sometimes gets a bad rap
15 Waste producer
16 Penetrated
18 Crystal user, perhaps
22 Simple melody
25 Handle
26 Opposite of 5-Across
27 Give a hand
28 Top
29 Nobel winner Wiesel
30 Importunes
31 It might be called

DOWN

1 Set up
2 Peres's predecessor
3 *Wheel of Fortune* category
4 *Decisions for a Decade* author
5 Mini munchie
6 Island entertainer
7 Bustles
8 Fielding requirement
9 Affectation
17 Some rockets
19 Wine label name
20 Send, one way
21 Parry
22 Racetrack sound
23 One was lost on April 5, 1998
24 Companion of the Charleses

13

Answer, page 426

ACROSS

1 Filch
4 Tank top?
10 Discoverer's reaction
11 Not out
12 It's torn from a roll
14 Gray of TV
15 *Narcissus and Goldmund* author
16 Keanu's costar, once
18 Fighting
23 Hungarian-born conductor
27 Vaudeville singer Bayes
28 It opens on Ogygia
30 Admission
31 Computer add-on?
32 Conundrums
33 Georgia, once: Abbr.

DOWN

1 Deals with it
2 Butler's desire
3 Visit
4 Long-jawed swimmer
5 Besides
6 Word with box or string
7 Female elephants
8 National Animal Disease Laboratory setting
9 Scorer of 1,281 goals
13 It can be loose or tight
17 Light, fast warship
19 Switch settings
20 Prescribed amounts
21 Drag need
22 "When I Need You" singer
23 Part of a flight
24 Cry of dread
25 "Shall we?" answer
26 Split
29 "Shall we?" answer

14

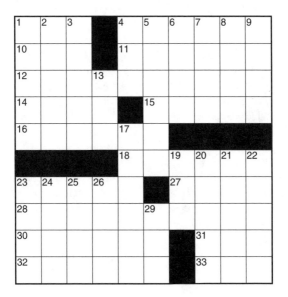

Answer, page 426

ACROSS

1 Adventurer Buntline
4 "Grand" island
10 See 1-Down
11 Best Picture of 1968
12 Buster
13 Capybara, e.g.
14 Abu Dhabi, for example
16 Doctor's order
17 He was Ali in *Lawrence of Arabia*
21 Jackie's favorite designer
22 Semblance
23 Fed-up cry
25 Puts in order
28 John's *Pulp Fiction* costar
29 Mingo's portrayer
30 Become soaking wet
31 Fair
32 Leading lady?

DOWN

1 With 10-Across, first
2 Dentin protector
3 Tractable
4 Cleaning compound
5 Heaps
6 Den of iniquity
7 Park, for one: Abbr.
8 Y chromosome carriers
9 Best Play of 1998
15 Nominee for Best Musical of 1998
18 Malapropism, for example
19 *The Caves of Steel* author
20 Make a new record of
22 Full of empty talk
24 Obedience school command
25 Gumshoe
26 Oath phrase
27 Obstruct

15

Answer, page 427

ACROSS

1 Obfuscation
4 "Zadok, the Priest" composer
10 No-trump winner
11 Kid-lit moppet
12 Golden Grand Slam winner
14 Bit of ideology
15 Subject of a Steve Martin song
16 Dignified
19 Painter Manet
23 Start of a series
26 Take in, perhaps
27 It's controlled from above
30 Dodona had a famous one
31 Ethan Allen's brother
32 Finn's friend
33 Gene's partner, at times

DOWN

1 Imitates Gandhi, perhaps
2 Beethoven's Opus 103, e.g.
3 Susan's 1991 costar
4 Tested the weight of
5 Clay, eventually
6 December concoction
7 Tabloid fodder
8 Son of Rebekah
9 It's just not right
13 Entertain
17 Temporary replacement
18 Log type
20 It's over many people's heads
21 What a hung jury forces a court to do
22 Frightful
23 Joel's follower
24 *When a Woman Sins* star
25 Sticking place?
28 None too friendly
29 Cheer for Manolete

16

Answer, page 427

ACROSS

1 Shoot
4 Spit in the food?
10 Mass conclusion
11 Make it
12 The constellation Reticulum
13 Driver in movies
14 Philosophies
16 Junior's senior
17 Actor Stephen
18 Liquor glass
19 Puff pieces?
21 Gee opposite
22 Bush was one
23 Literary middle name
26 Punch ingredient, perhaps
28 "Wait a second!"
29 Folded food
30 It's picked out
31 Most irritated
32 Fill out

DOWN

1 Calamine constituent
2 Maintain
3 Tongue twister subject
4 It's midway between Honolulu and Sydney
5 Barbra's 1976 costar
6 West end
7 Browse
8 Town on Lake Geneva
9 Reminiscent of the oboe, perhaps
15 Plaines leader
18 Dance step
19 Takebacks
20 "Cottonwood," in Spanish
21 "Grand" hotel
23 Seeds often get them
24 Eileithyia's mother
25 Examined
27 Flagon filler

1	2	3	⬛	4	5	6	7	8	9
10			⬛	11					
12			⬛	13					
14			15			⬛	16		
⬛		17			⬛	18			
19	20			⬛	21			⬛	⬛
22			⬛	23				24	25
26			27			⬛	28		
29						⬛	30		
31						⬛	32		

Answer, page 428

ACROSS

1 Program's prerelease version
5 Coach
10 Airline to the Middle East
11 Where the Temple of the Trung Sisters is
12 Scrambled
13 Kind of horizon
14 Coating material
16 Rams fans?
17 A pangram contains all of them
19 Super Bowl XVIII winners
23 Person who went through with an engagement
26 Wrinkle-resistant material
27 Out of sorts?
29 *Three Sisters* sister
30 Entrance
31 Landing place
32 Cheats at kriegspiel
33 Wizened

DOWN

1 Nut variety
2 Band on the run?
3 It has 78 cards
4 He played himself in *White Men Can't Jump*
5 Start of several Shakespeare titles
6 Does some spying
7 All over
8 Volcano feature
9 They're on the charts
15 Word of support
18 Carnival place
20 *It Happened One Night* character
21 Sessions of music
22 Percussion item
23 Contort
24 Rival of Bjorn
25 Word containing its own Roman equivalent
28 "___ Magic" (1948 song)

18

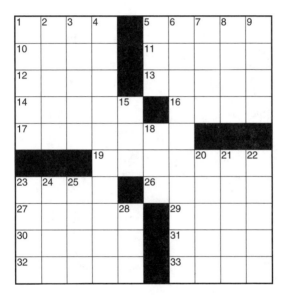

Answer, page 428

ACROSS

1 Bedouin, mainly
7 Pawns and such
10 Muhammad unified it
11 Flamenco cry
12 Mom or Dad
14 Use a letter opener
15 Rationed
16 Indistinct
17 "A Modest Proposal," e.g.
21 Far from awkward
22 Touched
26 Steptoeville, later
28 Journalist Curie
29 Controverted
30 Port, for example
31 Conditions

DOWN

1 Is off-guard
2 Kind of history
3 Bamako's land
4 Somewhat
5 Uproar
6 It has a pommel and a cantle
7 Simoleons
8 Bugs chaser
9 Codependent
13 Famous litigant
16 Part of the food pyramid's base
17 Carpenter, at times
18 Tequila source
19 Like some floors
20 Adverse
22 *Two Years Before the Mast* writer
23 Got down
24 Clear out
25 Small amounts
27 Serving alcohol

19

Answer, page 429

ACROSS

1 Became less intense
7 Binge
10 Rag
11 Be obligated to
12 Zest of a sort
14 Tender spot?
15 Poetic preposition
16 It can replace many items
18 *Imperial March* composer
22 Arrive
24 Baum creation
25 Soccer ___ (term used in 1996 elections)
27 Car cover
28 Best buddies?
32 Gun
33 Orpheus was one
34 Cut off
35 Peter, Paul, and Mary

DOWN

1 Brick materials
2 Upbraid
3 Famous landing place
4 Tenth anniversary gift, traditionally
5 Finish the yardwork
6 Man of cultivation
7 Country singer Diffie
8 Wonder
9 Salon selection
13 Hide
17 Offshoot
19 Kobold
20 Unmoving
21 Martin activities
23 Winter airs
26 Chiapas native
28 La leader
29 Charm
30 First lady
31 Cycle's start

20

Answer, page 429

Checker Puzzles

Robert Pike

Hints on pages 385–386
Answers on pages 430–443

INTRODUCTION

All sorts of puzzles provide fascinating fun for problem solvers, as evidenced by their widespread popularity in books, magazines, and newspapers. It is the author's hope that these checker puzzles will do the same for the readers of this book. There is an added dimension of universality with these problems and their solutions, since practically everyone knows how to play checkers, which is not the case with any other similar leisure-time activity.

In some cases you may want to check the hint section on pages 385–386. In other situations you might need to refer to the answer. But don't give up too easily—there is a winning solution to each problem in no more than five turns by the player who goes first. All the plays for both sides are forced by that player, who can definitely win by making the correct sequence of moves.

There are only five rules that need to be followed in working with these exercises:

1. If there is a jumping/capturing opportunity, it must be taken.
2. If there is more than one jumping opportunity available, any one may be taken.

3. When a player moves or jumps into his king row with a checker, his turn ends (he cannot continue and jump back out even if a jump is available).
4. Only kings can move and jump backward as well as forward.
5. Games are won by capturing all of the opponent's pieces or by blocking them so they can't move or jump anywhere when it's their turn to go.

Although many checker games end up in a draw, all of these puzzles have a winning solution, because it's more fun to win. In actual games, the best players always consider moves that will lead to a tie as well as a victory, since a tie is obviously better than a loss. In all of these problems the starting side (who should emerge triumphant) rarely has more manpower than the opponent and quite often has fewer checkers/kings—which makes the puzzles all the more exciting.

Some of the solutions fall short of an absolute victory as described above. Once a clear superiority of forces has been achieved by the solver, it is assumed that that player will not make a foolish mistake in the relatively simple cleanup operation required to complete the conquest—so the win is assumed.

1. Black Recovers Beautifully

Black is to move and he's down four to five in man-power. He makes two great plays to pull it out of the fire and emerge victorious. What are Black's tactics?

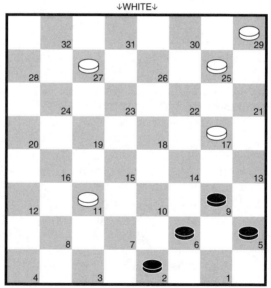

2. Black Magic

It's Black's turn to go in what seems to be an evenly matched contest, but Black makes it a quick game with a few deft moves. What are they?

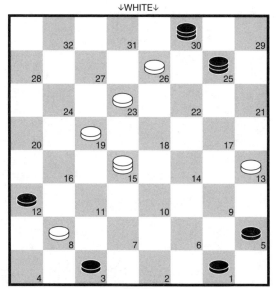

3. Black's Thinking Leaves White Blinking

Black's behind seven to eight, but it's his move and he finds a way to more than make up for the deficit and win the game. How does he do it?

4. White's Wishes Come True

Black has gotten careless in an unnecessary rush to obtain a lot of kings. It's White's move and he figures out an unusual way to make Black pay, and White wins the match. Can you follow the same victorious course?

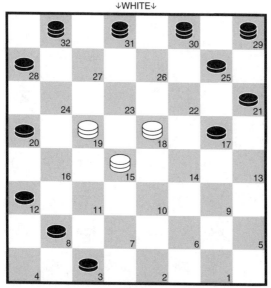

5. The Pale Forces Push Black Around

In this innocent-looking lineup, White has the move and makes a super series of plays to come out on top. How does he start and finish Black off?

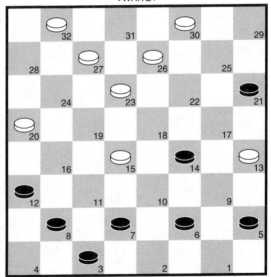

6. Black Turns the Table on White

It's Black's turn and he turns White's threat to jump into a quick but not-so-obvious win with some plays that wreak havoc with White's well-laid plans (not laid well enough). What is Black's upsetting strategy?

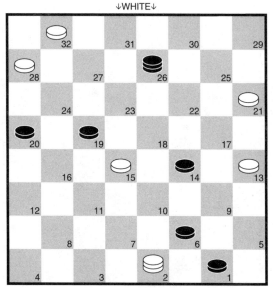

↓WHITE↓

↑BLACK↑

7. Black's Down, but Not Out

The dark forces are in a deficit situation from the standpoint of checker power and kings, but it's Black's turn to go and he makes the most of it. By the time White realizes what's happened, he has lost the contest to a very inventive challenger. How does Black manage this remarkable reversal?

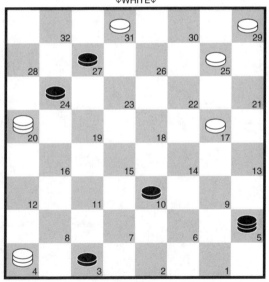

8. Another Comeback for Black

It's Black's move, but it looks like White is going to get a second and third king very quickly. Black turns that potential problem into a game-winning opportunity with some magnificent plays. What are they?

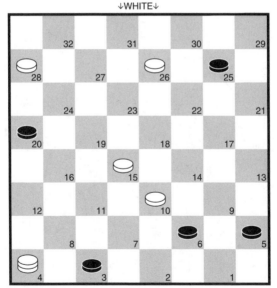

9. White Sees the Light

White is to move in this setup with Black ahead nine to eight in checker power. But not for long, as White sees the light at the end of the tunnel and pulls off a spectacular victory. How does he engineer this?

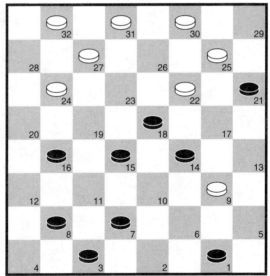

10. Black Makes Some Tricky Winning Moves

Black to move. He doesn't appear to be well positioned in this scenario, but he analyzes the situation carefully and comes up with an unstoppable game-winning series of strategic plays. Can you do the same?

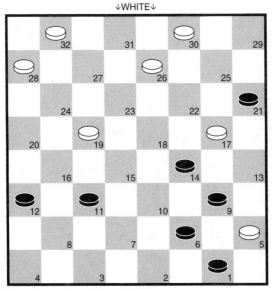

↓WHITE↓

↑BLACK↑

11. White Takes a Winning Flight

It looks like a difficult, evenly matched contest, but it's White's turn and he takes off with a fabulous series of plays to earn a well-deserved victory. What is White's flight plan?

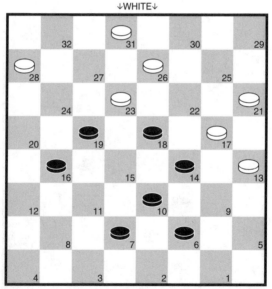

12. A Black Attack

Black goes on the offensive with his first move (although it seems crazy) to prevail in this marvelous example of strategy. What are Black's tactics?

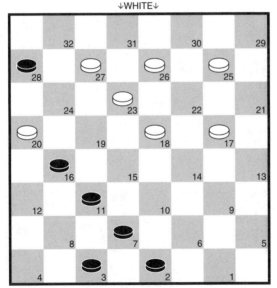

13. White Won't Quit

White seems to be hopelessly behind in material and at a positional disadvantage as well. He makes his turn to move first count for an incredible win. What does this most resilient of players do?

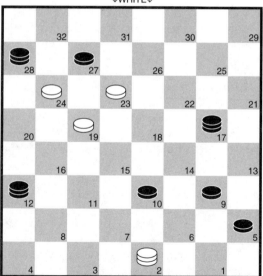

14. Black's Fantastic

White's way ahead in this situation with Black to move. Black uses it to his very best advantage and pulls off a stunning victory. Can you pull the same triggers on the stun gun?

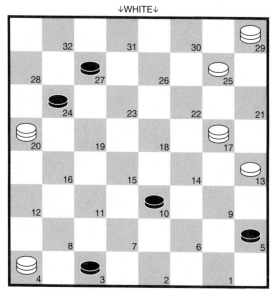

15. Black Plays Well to Win

It's seven up and Black's move with White threatening to jump the Black checker on 9. Black doesn't panic and uses great foresight to establish a winning position that scuttles the White ship. Can you chart the same course?

↓WHITE↓

↑BLACK↑

16. Black Shatters White's Hopes

It's Black's move and he finds the groove that turns a six-to-seven manpower deficit into a punishing positional win against an astonished White army. Can you emulate Black's super strategic play?

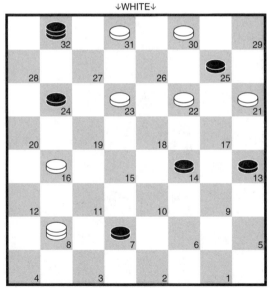

17. Black Works Wonders

It's Black's turn and his moves, in an apparently even game, are beautiful to everyone but White, who suddenly loses to Black's special strategy. Do you see what it is?

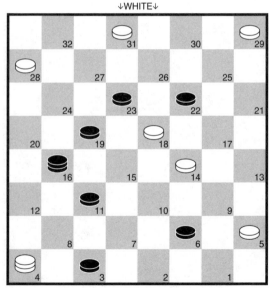

18. Black Storms Back

It's Black's turn and he completely confuses White with some preliminarily incomprehensible plays that, as they unfold, show White being put in an untenable position. How does Black accomplish this?

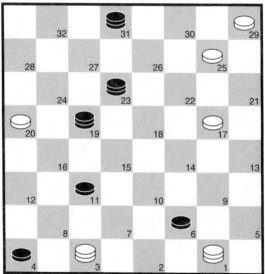

19. White Paves a Winning Way

It's White's turn. He employs it and the ones to follow to turn this even-looking game into a fun-filled victory march. What's White's parade route?

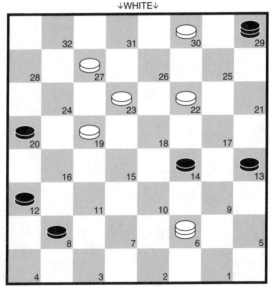

20. Black Makes White Turn Pale

Black's behind six to seven, but it's his move and he baffles White with an amazing series of plays that pulls the game out of the hat for an absolutely incredible win. Can you extract the same results from the hat?

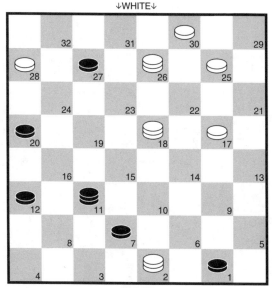

21. Farsighted Play Wins for Black

White is two kings ahead with Black to move, and Black moves so well that he garners a surprising victory over his unsuspecting opponent. How'd he do it?

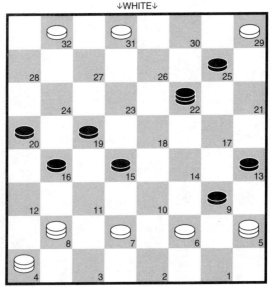

22. Black Gives White Fits

It's Black's turn and he appears to be in dire straits. A long-range thought process allows him to engineer a spectacular triumph. Can you build the same series of winning bridges?

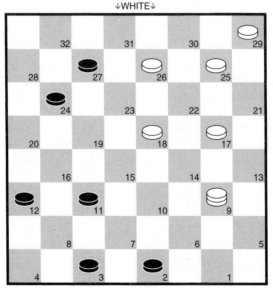

23. A Master Class Performance by Black

Black is to move and he does so masterfully in an outstanding display of checker acumen. If you can solve this one, you are in the same master class. Good hunting!

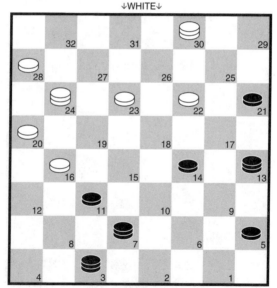

24. White Fashions a Spectacular Win

It looks almost hopeless for White in this setup where he's seriously outgunned. But he takes the maximum advantage of having the first turn by starting off a pyrotechnic sequence of jumps that culminate in an unforgettable victory. Can you light off the same fuse?

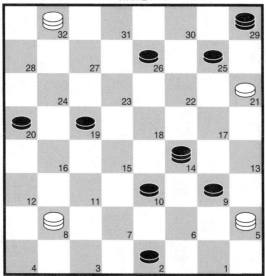

↓WHITE↓

↑BLACK↑

25. A Bright White Win

Here's what seems to be another equal match, but not for long after White, who goes first, spots a devastating series of winning moves. What are they?

26. Black Smites White

Black has less checker power than White, but it's his turn and he makes some plays that lead to a dramatic victory. What are they?

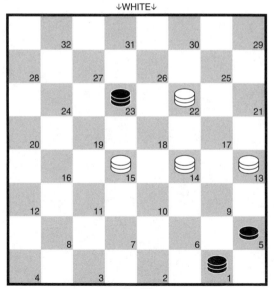

27. Fireworks for Six

It's Black's turn, and he's so far behind that he almost surrenders before finding a brilliant way to win. What is it?

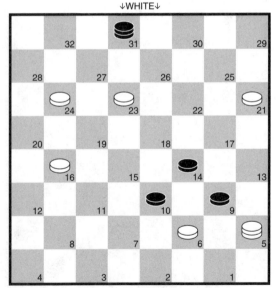

28. Black Seizes the Moment

White has advanced his checkers closer to his king row than Black, but not as cautiously as he should have. Black, who has the move, makes White pay dearly for forging ahead so recklessly. What does Black see and do?

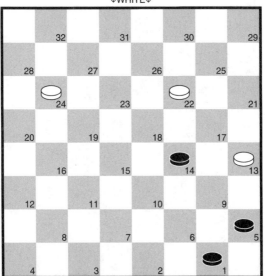

29. White's Inferior Forces Are Not a Deterrent

White's in desperate shape, but it's his turn and he doesn't despair as he makes a play that spoils Black's day. What could it be?

↓WHITE↓

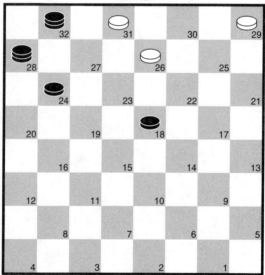

↑BLACK↑

30. Black Finds a Tiebreaker

It's Black's move and he can easily play to a draw. But suddenly he sees a way to win instead. Can you leap to the same conclusion?

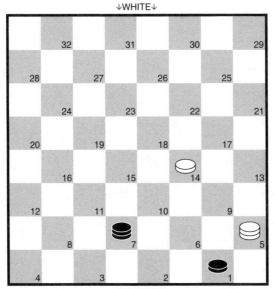

31. White Skins the Black Cat

White's move under fire turns out to be a game-winner in very short order. Can you find the right White strategy?

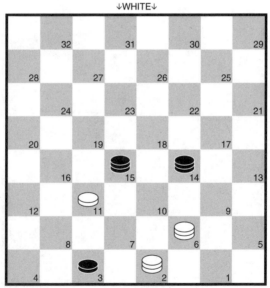

32. Black Has the Will and the Way to Win

It's Black's move in what could become a tie game unless Black can figure out a way to win. He does so, to White's dismay. What are the plays that do White in?

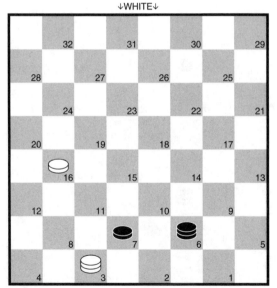

33. Black's Timing Leaves White Whining

It's Black's turn to go in this equal-looking contest. Black sees a different outcome with his team emerging victorious and makes the moves that make it happen. What are they?

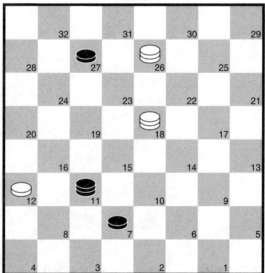

Brain Bafflers

Tim Sole & Rod Marshall

Answers on pages 444–452

1. What word, expression, or name is depicted below?

FAREDCE

Answer, page 444

2. What is the smallest integer that can be expressed as the sum of two squares in three different ways? The answer is less than 500.

Answer, page 444

3. One for the children: Would you rather a tiger chased you or a zebra?

Answer, page 444

4. When the examination results were published, one college found that all 32 of its students were successful in at least one of the three exams that each of them had taken. Of the students who did not pass Exam One, the number who passed Exam Two was exactly half of the number who passed Exam Three. The number who passed only Exam One was the same as the number who passed only one of the other two exams, and three more than the number who passed Exam One and at least one of the other two exams.

How many students passed more than one exam?

Answer, page 444

5. What word, expression, or name is depicted below?

Answer, page 444

6. Using exactly two 2s and any of the standard mathematical symbols, write down an expression whose value is five.

Answer, page 444

7. This puzzle was devised by Dr. Karl Fabel and published in 1949 in "T.R.D.'s Diamond Jubilee" issue of the *Fairy Chess Review*.

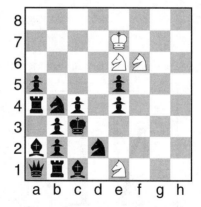

White to play and mate in sixty.

Answer, pages 444–446

8. What word, expression, or name is depicted below?

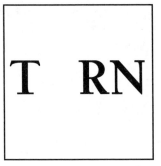

Answer, page 446

9. Find a ten-digit number whose first digit is the number of ones in the number, whose second digit is the number of twos in the number, whose third digit is the number of threes in the number, and so on up to the tenth digit, which is the number of zeros in the number.

Answer, page 446

10. Without using a calculator, guess which is bigger: e^{π} or π^{e}?

Answer, page 446

11. A selection of eight cards is dealt with every second card being returned to the bottom of the pack. Thus the top card goes to the table, card two goes to the bottom of the pack, card three goes to the table, card four to the bottom of the pack, and so on. This procedure continues until all the cards are dealt.

The order in which the cards appear on the table is:

A K A K A K A K

How were the cards originally stacked?

Answer, page 446

12. At the end of the soccer season, every player had scored a prime number of goals and the average for the eleven players was also a prime number. No player's tally was the same as anyone else's, and neither was it the same as the average.

Given that nobody had scored more than 45 goals, how many goals did each player score?

Answer, page 446

13. Gambler A chooses a series of three possible outcomes from successive throws of a die, depending simply on whether the number thrown each time is odd (O) or even (E). Gambler B then chooses a different series of three successive possible outcomes. The die is then thrown as often as necessary until either gambler's chosen series of outcomes occurs.

For example, Gambler A might choose the series EOE and B might choose OEE. If successive throws gave, say, EEOOEOE, then A would win the game after the seventh throw. Had the sixth throw been E rather than O, then B would have won.

A has chosen the series EEE and B, who was thinking of choosing OEE, changes his mind to OOO. Has B reduced his chance of winning the game or is it still the same?

Answer, page 446

14. Find three different two-digit primes where the average of any two is a prime and the average of all three is a prime.

Answer, page 447

15. What word, expression, or name is depicted below?

Answer, page 447

16. In a game of table tennis, 24 of the 37 points played were won by the player serving, and Smith beat Jones 21–16. Remembering in table tennis that service alternates every five points, who served first?

Answer, page 447

17. This chess puzzle by C.S. Kipping was published in the *Manchester City News* in 1911.

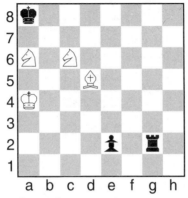

White to play and mate in three.

Answer, pages 447–448

18. Caesar and Brutus are playing a game in which each says the next number from a well-known sequence. The first 20 terms of the sequence are given below:

1 2 3 2 1 2 3 4 2 1 2 3 4 3 2 3 4 5 3 2

The fortieth term is 2. If Caesar began the game, who will be the first to say 10?

Answer, page 448

19. What word, expression, or name is depicted below?

EVER
EVER
EVER
EVER
EVER

Answer, page 448

20. Find nine different integers from 1 to 20 inclusive such that no combination of any three of the nine integers form an arithmetic progression. For example, if two of the integers chosen were 7 and 13, then that would preclude 1, 10, and 19 from being included.

Answer, page 448

21. Two travelers set out at the same time to travel opposite ways round a circular railway. Trains start each way every 15 minutes, on the hour, 15 minutes past, half past, and 45 minutes past. Clockwise trains take two hours for the journey, counterclockwise trains take three hours. Including trains seen at the starting point and the ones they are traveling on, how many trains does each traveler see on his journey?

Answer, page 448

22. What word, expression, or name is depicted below?

Answer, page 448

23. This puzzle was composed by Hans August and Dr. Karl Fabel, and was published in 1949 in *Romana de Sah*.

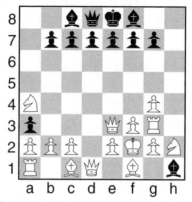

White has just made his seventeenth move. What was Black's ninth move, and what were the moves that followed it?

Answer, page 449

24. There is one in a minute and two in a moment, but only one in a million years. What are we talking about?

Answer, page 450

25. A drawer contains a number of red and blue socks. If I pull two out at random, then the chance of them being a red pair is a half and the chance of them being a blue pair is a twelfth. How many socks are in the drawer?

Answer, page 450

26. What word, expression, or name is depicted below?

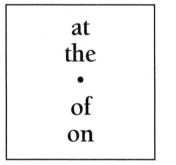

Answer, page 450

27. We place in a box 13 white marbles and 15 black. We also have 28 black marbles outside the box.

We remove two marbles from the box. If they have a different color, we put the white one back in the box. If they have the same color, we put a black marble in the box. We continue doing this until only one marble is left in the box. What is its color?

Answer, page 450

28. A long time ago, you could buy eight hens for a dollar or one sheep for a dollar, and cows were ten dollars each. A farmer buying animals of each type bought a hundred animals for a hundred dollars. What animals did he buy?

Answer, page 450

29. Insert the missing letter:

J ? M A M J J A

Answer, page 450

30. What word, expression, or name is depicted below?

Answer, page 450

31. Find two ten-digit numbers, each containing the digits from 0 to 9 once and once only, with the property that successive pairs of digits, from left to right, are divisible in turn by 2, 3, 4, 5, 6, 7, 8, 9, and 10.

Answer, page 450

32. Lynsey is a biology student. Her project for this term is measuring the effect of an increase in vitamin C in the diet of 25 laboratory mice. Each mouse will have a different diet supplement of between 1 to 50 units. Fractions of a unit are not possible.

Although the university pays for the mice's food, Lynsey has to buy the vitamin C supplement herself. The first consideration in designing this experiment is therefore to minimize the total number of supplements.

The second consideration is that no mouse should have an exact multiple of another mouse's supplement. Thus, if one mouse is on a supplement of 14 units, then this will preclude supplements of 1, 2, 7, 28, and 42 units.

What supplements should Lynsey use?

Answer, page 450

33. "Strength" is an eight-letter word with only one vowel. What's an eight-letter word with five vowels in a row?

Answer, page 451

34. Are 1997 nickels worth more than 1992 nickels?

Answer, page 451

35. What word, expression, or name is depicted below?

STEP
PETS
PETS

Answer, page 451

36. The number 6 has factors (not counting itself) of 1, 2, and 3, which add up to 6. The number 28 has the same property, since its factors, 1, 2, 4, 7, and 14, add up to 28. What four-digit number has this property?

Answer, page 451

37. What is the next term in this series:

1248   1632   6412   8256   ?

Answer, page 451

38. What word, expression, or name is depicted below?

Answer, page 451

39. A set of building blocks contains a number of wooden cubes. The six faces of each cube are painted, each with a single color, in such a way that no two adjacent faces have the same color. Given that only five different colors have been used and that no two of the blocks are identical in their colorings, what is the maximum number of blocks there can be in the set?

Answer, pages 451–452

40. The Bowls Club has fewer than 100 members. To the nearest whole number, 28% of the members are former committee members, 29% are current committee members, and 42% have never been on the committee. Again to the nearest whole number, 35% of the former committee members are women. What is the total membership of the club?

Answer, page 452

41. The pars for a nine-hole golf course designed by a mathematician are:

   3   3   5   4   4   3   5   5   4

On which very well-known series (as well-known as one, two, three, etc.) are the pars based?

Answer, page 452

42. This may seem self-contradictory, but find three integers in arithmetic progression (that is, with equal differences, such as 230, 236, and 242) whose product is prime.

Answer, page 452

43. The ages of Old and Young total 48. Old is twice as old as Young was when Old was half as old as Young will be when Young is three times as old as Old was when Old was three times as old as Young. How old is Old?

Answer, page 452

44. What word, expression, or name is depicted below?

Answer, page 452

Puzzles for Word Lovers

George Bredehorn

Answers on pages 453–472

DIRECTIONS
• • • • • • • • • • • • •

CLUELESS CROSSWORDS
Fill in the blanks in the grid so that eight seven-letter words are formed.

FILL-IN STATION
Fill in the grid with the nine letters given below it so that three-letter words are formed in all the directions that the arrows point.

LATTICEWORK
Fill in the blanks so that the words interlock and fit the category given above the grid.

MIXAGRAMS
Each line contains a five-letter word and a four-letter word whose letters have been mixed, but the left-to-right order of the letters has not been changed. Unmix the two words on each line and write them in the spaces provided. When you're done, the answer to the clue will appear in the two marked columns.
Example: D A R I U N V E T = DRIVE + AUNT

TWO BY TWO

Only two different letters are needed to complete each of these miniature crisscross puzzles. All the vowels have been placed for you. Pick two consonants and repeat them as often as necessary to finish each grid. No words are repeated in any one puzzle, and no proper names, hyphenated words, or words containing apostrophes are used.

TWO BY TWO

Directions, page 277   *Answer, pages 453–454*

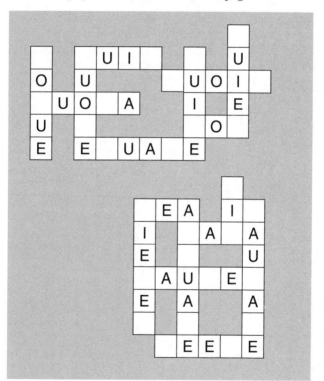

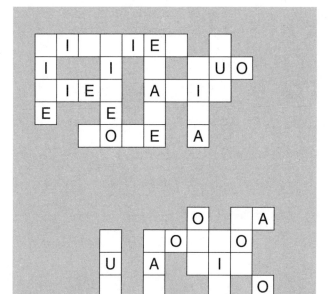

MIXAGRAMS

Directions, page 276   *Answer, page 454*

 1

Clue: Stool pigeon, perhaps

↓   ↓

D E S H B U S H T = _ _ _ _ _ + _ _ _ _

S E D C R I T O D = _ _ _ _ _ + _ _ _ _

A G O M R E N E D = _ _ _ _ _ + _ _ _ _

U S E N A D G E S = _ _ _ _ _ + _ _ _ _

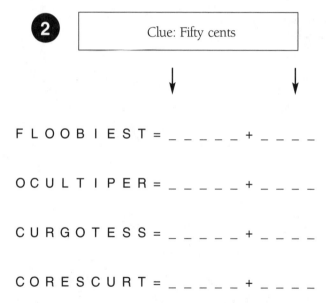

2 Clue: Fifty cents

F L O O B I E S T = _ _ _ _ _ + _ _ _ _

O C U L T I P E R = _ _ _ _ _ + _ _ _ _

C U R G O T E S S = _ _ _ _ _ + _ _ _ _

C O R E S C U R T = _ _ _ _ _ + _ _ _ _

TWO BY TWO

Directions, page 277   *Answer, pages 455–456*

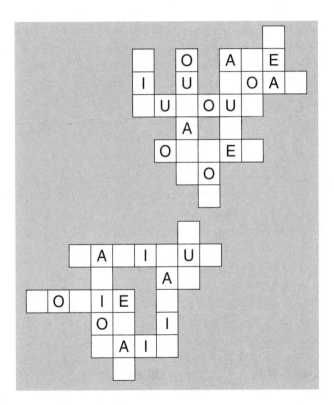

Directions, page 276   *Answer, page 457*

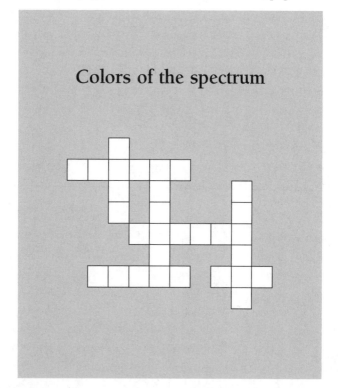

Colors of the spectrum

Planets in our solar system

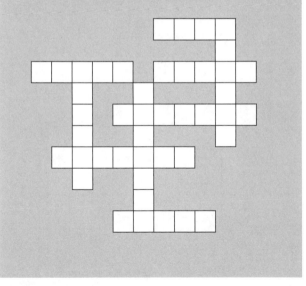

TWO BY TWO

Directions, page 277

Answer, pages 458–459

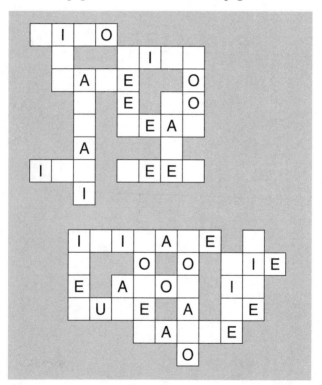

MIXAGRAMS

Directions, page 276   *Answer, page 460*

Clue: It's needed after the bell

↓   ↓

P A W C H O R E L = _ _ _ _ _ + _ _ _ _

A B A L L S E A S = _ _ _ _ _ + _ _ _ _

S A B L E G E A T = _ _ _ _ _ + _ _ _ _

S T E N O S E A P = _ _ _ _ _ + _ _ _ _

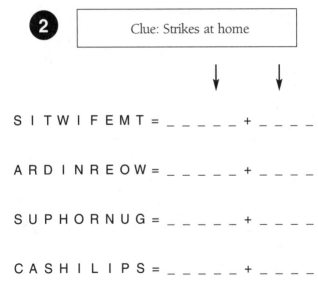

2   Clue: Strikes at home

S I T W I F E M T = _ _ _ _ _ + _ _ _ _

A R D I N R E O W = _ _ _ _ _ + _ _ _ _

S U P H O R N U G = _ _ _ _ _ + _ _ _ _

C A S H I L I P S = _ _ _ _ _ + _ _ _ _

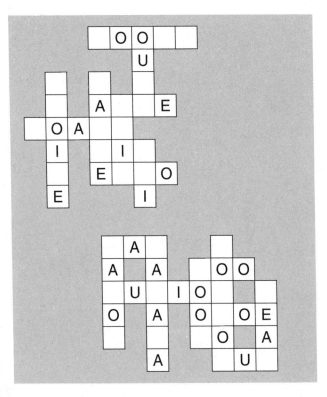

MIXAGRAMS

Directions, page 276   *Answer, page 462*

 Clue: Music or marble

E T R I C H I C E = _ _ _ _ _ + _ _ _ _

C R O N A T O N E = _ _ _ _ _ + _ _ _ _

T O R C H S O W O = _ _ _ _ _ + _ _ _ _

R A K D A R I N G = _ _ _ _ _ + _ _ _ _

2 | Clue: Where you may turn to port

↓   ↓

S L O W H E R O D = _ _ _ _ _ + _ _ _ _

H A L O I G O N D = _ _ _ _ _ + _ _ _ _

F O G E N C R E E = _ _ _ _ _ + _ _ _ _

A P I D E P E R T = _ _ _ _ _ + _ _ _ _

FILL-IN STATION

Directions, page 276   *Answer, page 462*

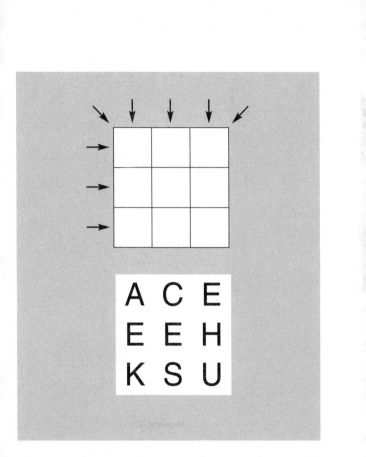

TWO BY TWO

Directions, page 277   Answer, pages 463–464

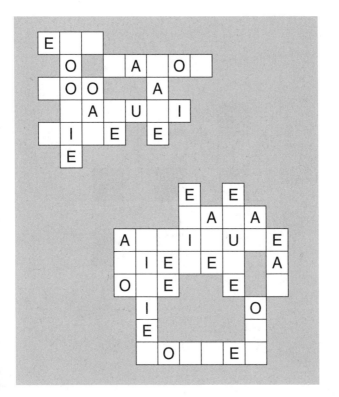

CLUELESS CROSSWORDS

Directions, page 276 *Answer, page 465*

MIXAGRAMS

Directions, page 276   *Answer, page 466*

Clue: Training regiment

A N T E R W A C K = _ _ _ _ _ + _ _ _ _

C H E O U R O P E = _ _ _ _ _ + _ _ _ _

L A P P O S O R E = _ _ _ _ _ + _ _ _ _

P A D E D L E A K = _ _ _ _ _ + _ _ _ _

2

Clue: Kind of cake

↓ ↓

G A S P U Z O T E = _ _ _ _ _ + _ _ _ _

B O V E R A L E T = _ _ _ _ _ + _ _ _ _

B R A B U S E T H = _ _ _ _ _ + _ _ _ _

P U P T O O T L Y = _ _ _ _ _ + _ _ _ _

TWO BY TWO

Directions, page 277　　　　　*Answer, pages 466–468*

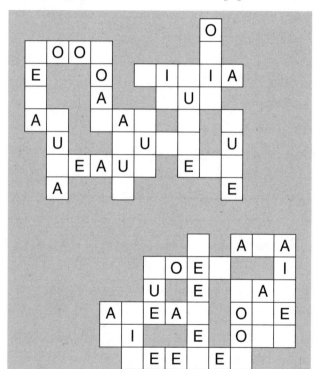

Directions, page 276   *Answer, pages 468–469*

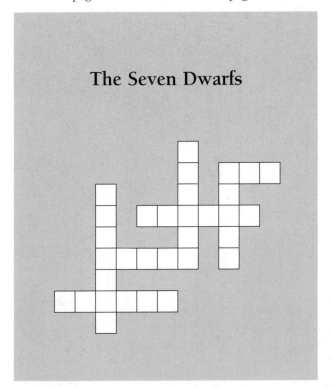

The Seven Dwarfs

U.S. Presidents from 1950 to 2000

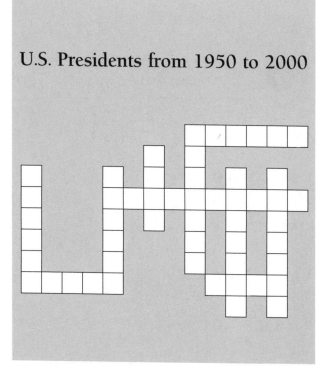

MIXAGRAMS

Directions, page 276

Answer, page 469

1

Clue: Turkey choice

↓   ↓

T C L O H U D E M = _ _ _ _ _ + _ _ _ _

K A M P I P A T E = _ _ _ _ _ + _ _ _ _

A R A L T I A R A = _ _ _ _ _ + _ _ _ _

S A B U P T O O K = _ _ _ _ _ + _ _ _ _

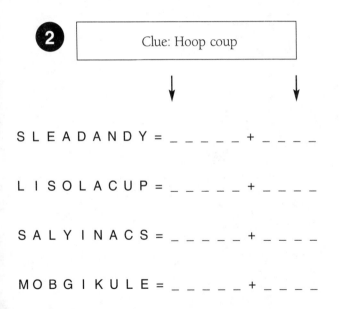

2

Clue: Hoop coup

S L E A D A N D Y = _ _ _ _ _ + _ _ _ _

L I S O L A C U P = _ _ _ _ _ + _ _ _ _

S A L Y I N A C S = _ _ _ _ _ + _ _ _ _

M O B G I K U L E = _ _ _ _ _ + _ _ _ _

FILL-IN STATION

Directions, page 276 *Answer, page 469*

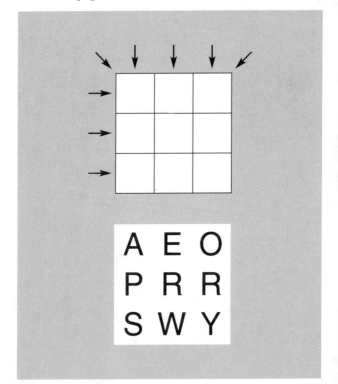

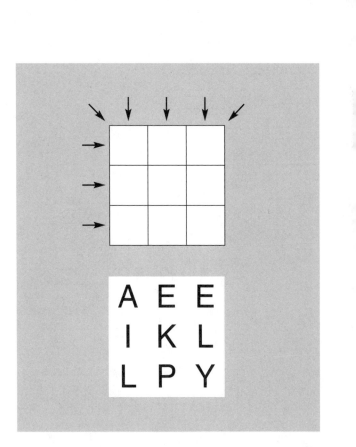

309

TWO BY TWO

Directions, page 277   *Answer, pages 470–471*

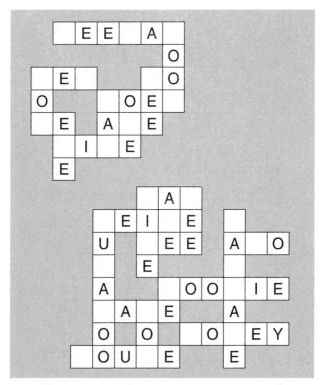

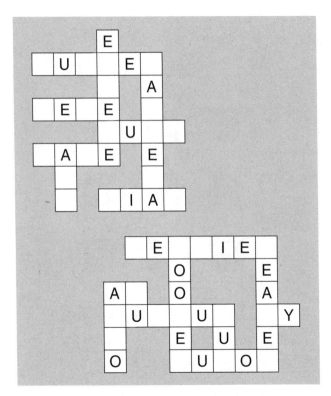

CLUELESS CROSSWORDS

Directions, page 276

Answer, page 472

Quick-to-Solve Brainteasers

J.J. Mendoza Fernández

Answers on pages 473–488

1

How many times can you subtract 6 from 30?

2

What number can you subtract half from to obtain a result that is zero?

3

How can half of 12 be 7?

4

Find two positive numbers that have a one-digit answer when multiplied and a two-digit answer when added.

5

Find two whole, positive numbers that have the same answer when multiplied together as when one is divided by the other.

6

Find two positive numbers that have the same answer when multiplied together as when added together.

7

Find a two-digit number that equals two times the result of multiplying its digits.

8

Find three whole, positive numbers that have the same answer when multiplied together as when added together.

9

What two two-digit numbers are each equal to their rightmost digit squared?

10

Find the highest number that can be written with three digits.

11

The ages of a father and a son add up to 55. The father's age is the son's age reversed. How old are they?

12

How much do 10 pieces of candy cost if one thousand pieces cost $10?

13

An outlet and a lightbulb cost $1.20. We know that the outlet costs $1 more than the lightbulb. How much does each cost?

14

If 75% of all women are tall, 75% are brunette, and 75% are pretty, what is the minimum percentage of tall, brunette, pretty women?

15

Thirty-two students took a nationwide exam and all the students from New York passed it. If the students from New York made up exactly 5% of the total number of the students that passed the test, how many students passed it and how many students were from New York?

16

Of the 960 people in a theater, 17% tipped 5 cents to the usher, 50% of the remaining 83% tipped 10 cents, and the rest tipped nothing. How much did the usher get?

17

What must you do to make the equation below true?
$$81 \times 9 = 801$$

18

There are 100 buildings along a street. A sign maker is ordered to number the buildings from 1 to 100. How many "9's" will he need?

19

How many tickets with different points of origination and destination can be sold on a bus line that travels a loop of 25 stops?

20

We know that humans have up to 100,000 hairs. In a city with more than 200,000 people, would it be possible to find two or more people with the same number of hairs?

21

All my ties are red except two. All my ties are blue except two. All my ties are brown except two. How many ties do I have?

22

A street that's 30 yards long has a chestnut tree every 6 yards on both sides. How many chestnut trees are on the entire street?

23

A pet shop owner is in the countryside. If he says, "one bird per olive tree," there is one bird too many.

However, if he says, "two birds per olive tree," there are no birds left over. How many birds and olive trees are there?

24

In a singles tennis tournament, 111 players participated. They used a new ball for each match. When a player lost one match, he was eliminated from the tournament. How many balls did they need?

25

Peter and John had a picnic. Peter had already eaten half of the muffins when John ate half of the remaining muffins plus three more. There were no muffins left. How many muffins did they take to the picnic?

26

A shepherd says to another, "If I give you one sheep, you will have twice the number of sheep that I have, but if you give me one, we will both have the same number of sheep." How many sheep did each shepherd have?

27

If I put in one canary per cage, I have one bird too many. However, if I put in two canaries per cage, I have one cage too many. How many cages and birds do I have?

28

If 1½ sardines cost 1½ dollars, how much would 7½ sardines cost?

29

If a brick weighs 3 pounds plus ½ a brick, what's the weight of 1½ bricks?

30

If 1½ dozen sardines costs 9½ dollars, how much do 18 sardines cost?

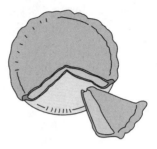

31

If 1½ men can eat 1½ pies in 1½ minutes, how many pies can 3 men eat in half an hour?

32

Yesterday afternoon, I went to visit my friend Albert, who is a painter. While I was watching him paint, I told him, "No wonder it takes you so long to finish a painting. Since I arrived, you have entered the studio twelve times." How many times did he leave the studio?

33

If two ducks are swimming in front of another duck, two ducks are swimming behind another duck, and one duck is swimming between two other ducks, what is the minimum number of ducks?

34

Two people were flipping coins. Each time, they bet $1 apiece. At the end, one person won $3 and the other one won three times. How many games did they play?

35

A bottle with a cylindrical shape at the bottom and with an irregular shape at the top is filled halfway to the top with liquid. The cylindrical part contains approximately three-fourths of the capacity of the bottle and we wish to determine the exact percentage of liquid that the bottle contains. We cannot open it and we can only use a ruler. What must we do?

36

If one nickel is worth five cents, how much is half of one half of a nickel worth?

37

Two soldiers have been ordered to do the following chores:

1. Peel potatoes.
2. Do the dishes.
3. Mow the lawn.

Each of these chores, when done by one person, takes one hour. If they start at 8 A.M., what could they do to take as little time as possible if they have only one knife, one lawn mower, and one sink with room for one person?

38

A spider spins its web in a window frame. Each day, it spins an area equal to that of the amount already completed. It takes 30 days to cover the entire window frame. How long would two spiders take? (In the case of two spiders, each of them spins an amount equal to the area of the existing part of the web made by that particular spider.)

39

We put a spore in a test tube. Every hour the spore divides into three parts, all the same size as the original part. If we put it in at 3 P.M., at 9 P.M. the tube will be completely full. At what time will the tube be one-third full?

40

How long is a rope that is 2 yards shorter than another rope that is three times the length of the first rope?

41

If a post is 6 yards longer than half of its own length, how long is the post?

42

How much mud (measured in liters) is there in a rectangular hole 2 meters wide, 3 meters long, and 3 meters deep?

43

One mother gave 25 books to her daughter and another mother gave her daughter 8 books. However, between both daughters they only increased their collection by 25 books. How can this be?

44

Emily is taller than Ann and shorter than Dolores. Who is the tallest of the three?

45

Rose is now as old as Joan was six years ago. Who is older?

46

If Emily speaks in a softer voice than Ann, and Dolores in a louder voice than Ann, does Emily speak louder or softer than Dolores?

47

James is sitting between John and Peter. Philip is sitting on Peter's right. Between whom is Peter sitting?

48

What has more value, one pound of $10 gold coins or half a pound of $20 gold coins?

49

A man went into a store and bought an umbrella for $10. He gave the salesperson a $50 bill. The salesperson went to the bank to get change. Two hours later, the bank teller went to the store claiming that the $50 bill was counterfeit, so the salesperson had to exchange it for a real one with the bank teller. Between the customer and the bank, how much did the store lose?

50

We have two pitchers, one with one quart of water and the other with one quart of wine. We take a tablespoon of the wine and mix it in the pitcher of water. Then we take a tablespoon from this pitcher and mix it into the pitcher with the wine. Is there more wine in the water pitcher or more water in the wine pitcher? What would have happened if, after pouring a spoonful of wine into the water, we had not mixed it well?

51

A sultan wanted to offer his daughter in marriage to the candidate whose horse would win the race. However, the rules of the race stated that the winner would be the one in last place. He didn't want the race to last forever, so he thought of a way to solve this. What was it?

52

On one side of a scale we have a partially filled fish-bowl. When we put a fish in the bowl, the total weight of the bowl increases by exactly the same as the weight of the fish. However, if we hold the fish by the tail and partially introduce it into the water, will the total weight be greater than before introducing the fish?

53

We have a scale and a set of weights in a field. The scale is not very accurate, but it is consistent in its inaccuracies. How can we know the exact weight of four apples?

54

A little bird weighing 5 ounces is sleeping in a cage. We put the cage on a scale and it weighs one pound. The bird then wakes up and starts flying all over the cage. What will the scale indicate while the bird is in the air?

55

We have 10 sacks full of balls. All sacks contain balls weighing 10 ounces each, except one of the sacks, which contains balls weighing 9 ounces each. By weighing the balls, what would be the minimum number of weighings required (on a scale that gives weight readouts) to identify the sack containing the defective balls?

56

Now we have 10 sacks that contain either 10-ounce balls or 9-ounce balls. Each sack has at least 1,000 balls, and all the balls in one sack are the same weight. However, we do not know how many sacks contain the

9-ounce balls or which ones they are. How can we identify these sacks by weighing the balls (on a scale that gives weight readouts) in the fewest number of tries?

57

I have six pieces of a chain, each piece made up of 4 links, and I want to make a single straight chain out of them. The blacksmith charges 10 cents for cutting each link and 50 cents for welding a link. How much will the chain cost?

58

A lady arrives at a hotel where rooms are $10 per night. When she checks in, she does not have enough money, but she offers to pay with a clasped gold bracelet. The bracelet has seven links, each valued at $10. What would be the fewest number of cuts necessary to let her stay for one week if she wants to pay one day at a time?

59

"And then I took out my sword and cut the thick chain that was linked to two posts into two pieces," said the samurai.

"That is not true," said the monk.

How did the monk know the samurai's story was untrue?

60

We have 10 glasses sitting in a row. The first five are filled with water and the other five are empty. What would be the minimum number of glasses needed to move so that the full and the empty glasses alternate?

61

In five plastic cups there are five marbles, each of different colors: white, black, red, green, and blue. We mark each cup randomly with the initial of one of the colors. If the white, green, red, and blue marbles are in their respective cups, how likely is it that the black marble is in its cup?

62

We have 8 pairs of white socks and 10 pairs of black socks in a box. What would be the minimum number of socks that we need to take out of the box to ensure that we get one pair of the same color? (Imagine that you cannot see the color when you are picking them from the box.)

63

We have 8 pairs of white socks, 9 pairs of black socks and 11 pairs of blue socks in a box. What would be the minimum number of socks that we need to take out of the box to ensure that we get one pair of the same color? (Imagine that you cannot see the color when you are picking them from the box.)

64

We have 6 pairs of white gloves and 6 pairs of black gloves in a box. What would be the minimum number of gloves that we need to take out of the box to ensure that we get one pair? (Imagine that you cannot see the color when you are picking them from the box.)

65

We have six white marbles, four black marbles, and one red marble in a box. What would be the least number of marbles that we need to take out of the box to ensure that we get three of the same color?

66

Distribute ten marbles in three plastic cups so that every cup contains an odd number of marbles. You must use all ten.

67

Distribute nine marbles in four boxes so that each box contains an odd number of marbles, different from the three other boxes. You must use all nine.

68

We have three boxes. One contains two black marbles, the second box contains two white marbles, and the third box contains one black and one white marble. The boxes are marked BB, WW, BW. However, no code corresponds with the marbles in its box. What would be the least number of marbles that must be randomly picked, from one or several boxes, to identify their contents?

69

A schoolteacher uses a five-hour hourglass to keep track of class time. One day, he sets the hourglass at 9 A.M. and while he is teaching his class, a student inadvertently inverts the hourglass. Another student, who notices this, sets the hourglass to its initial position at 11:30 A.M. In this way, the class ends at 3 P.M. At what time did the first student invert the hourglass?

70

A clock gains half a minute every day. Another clock doesn't work. Which one will show the correct time more often?

71

What time is it when a clock strikes 13 times?

72

In a conventional clock, how many times does the minute hand pass the hour hand between noon and midnight?

73

If a clock takes two seconds to strike 2, how long will it take to strike 3?

74

When I gave Albert a ride home, I noticed that the clock in his living room took 7 seconds to strike 8. I immediately asked him, "How long do I have to wait to hear it strike 12?"

75

A clock takes five seconds when striking 6. How long will it take when striking 12?

76

A Roman was born the first day of the 30th year before Christ and died the first day of the 30th year after Christ. How many years did he live?

77

On March 15, a friend was telling me, "Every day I have a cup of coffee. I drank 31 cups in January, 28 in February, and 15 in March. So far, I drank 74 cups of coffee. Do you know how many cups I would have drunk thus far if it had been a leap year?"

78

If yesterday had been Wednesday's tomorrow and tomorrow is Sunday's yesterday, what day would today be?

79

Mrs. Smith left on a trip the day after the day before yesterday and she will be back the eve of the day after tomorrow. How many days is she away?

80

A man was telling me on a particular occasion, "The day before yesterday I was 35 years old and next year I will turn 38." How can this be?

81

A famous composer blew out 18 candles on his birthday cake and then died less than nine months later. He was 76 at the time of his death and had composed *The Barber of Seville*. How could this happen?

82

Find a commonly used word that ends in T, contains the letters VEN, and starts with IN.

83

If you can speak properly, you will be able to answer the following question. Which is correct, "The yolk of an egg is white" or "The yolk of an egg are white"?

84

What is the opposite of "I AM NOT LEAVING"?

85

What 11-letter word is pronounced incorrectly by more than 99% of Ivy League graduates?

86

What 7-letter word becomes longer when the third letter is removed?

87

Five times four twenty, plus two, equals twenty-three. Is this true?

88

Paris starts with a "p" and ends with an "e." Is this true?

89

A phone conversation:

"May I speak to the director?"

"Who's calling?"

"John Rominch."

"I beg your pardon. Could you spell your last name?"

"R as in Rome, O as in Oslo, M as in Madrid, I as in Innsbruck ..."

"I as in what?"

"Innsbruck."

"Thanks. Please go ahead."

"N as in Nome ..."

This does not make sense. Why?

90

What can you always find in the middle of a taxicab?

91

Is the sentence "This statement is false" true or false?

92

What occurs once in June and twice in August, but never occurs in October?

93

"I must admit that I was not serious when I was telling you that I was not kidding about rethinking my decision of not changing my mind," my friend was telling me. So, is he really going to change his mind or not?

94

A criminal is sentenced to death. Before his execution, he is allowed to make a statement. If his statement is false, he will be hanged, and if his statement is true, he will be drowned. What should he say to confuse the jury and thus save his life?

95

A woman has five children and half of them are male. Is this possible?

96

A friend was telling me, "I have eight sons and each has one sister." In total, how many children does my friend have?

97

Ann's brother has one more brother than sisters. How many more brothers than sisters does Ann have?

98

"I have as many brothers as sisters, but my brothers have twice the number of sisters as brothers. How many of us are there?"

99

A doctor has a brother who is an attorney in Alabama, but the attorney in Alabama does not have a brother who is a doctor. How can this be?

100

John wonders, "If Raymond's son is my son's father, how am I related to Raymond?"

101

If your uncle's sister is related to you, but is not your aunt, what is the relation?

102

A group of paleontologists found a prehistoric cave and one of them is congratulated by a younger son, who writes a telegram to his dad explaining the discovery. Who discovered the cave?

103

The other day, I heard the following conversation:

"Charles is related to you the same way I am to your son."

"And you are related to me in the same way Charles is to you."

How are Charles and the second man related?

104

Can someone marry his brother's wife's mother-in-law?

105

Ann is looking at the portrait of a gentleman. "He is not my father, but his mother was my mother's mother-in-law," she says. Who is this gentleman?

106

Do you know if the Catholic Church allows a man to marry his widow's sister?

107

A friend of mine was looking at a photo when she said, "Brothers and sisters? I have one. And this man's father is my father's son." Who was in the photo?

108

A friend of mine was looking at a photo when he said, "Brother and sisters? I have none. But this man's son is my father's son." Who was in the photo?

109

Two women are talking on the street. When they see two men coming, they say, "There are our fathers, our mothers' husbands, our children's fathers, and our own husbands." How can you explain this?

Hard-to-Solve Brainteasers

Jaime & Lea Poniachik

Answers on pages 489–509

1. Twins

Peter and Paul are twin brothers. One of them (we don't know which) always lies. The other one always tells the truth. I ask one of them:

"Is Paul the one that lies?"

"Yes," he answers.

Did I speak to Peter or Paul?

2. Twin Statistics

Suppose that 3% of births give rise to twins. What percentage of the population is a twin: 3%, less than 3%, or more than 3%?

3. The Professor and His Friend

Professor Zizoloziz puts 40 matches on the table and explains a game to his friend Kathy.

Each player in turn takes 1, 3, or 5 matches. The winner is the one who takes the last match. Kathy chooses to go first and takes 3 matches.

Who do you think will win this game, Kathy or the professor?

4. Irregular Circuit

Two cars start from point A at the same time and drive around a circuit more than one mile in length. While they are driving laps around the circuit, each car must maintain a steady speed. Since one car is faster than the other, one car will pass the other at certain points. The first pass occurs 150 yards from point A.

At what distance from A will one car pass the other again?

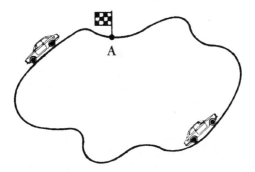

5. Economical Progression

Below are four terms in an arithmetic progression (a series in which the difference between terms is constant, in this case 50):

5, 55, 105, 155

Notice how the four terms use only three different digits: 0, 1, and 5.

Can you find six terms in an arithmetic progression that use only three different digits?

6. Skin and Shoes

A white man is wearing a pair of white shoes, a black man is wearing a pair of black shoes, and a red-skinned man is wearing a pair of red shoes. In a gesture of friendship, they decide to exchange shoes. When they are done, each man has on one shoe from each of the other two men.

How many shoes will you have to look at to know which color of shoe each man is wearing on each foot; that is, which color shoe each man wears on his right foot and which color each man wears on his left foot? Note that when you look at a shoe, you can see that man's skin color.

7. Up and Down

This morning I had to take the stairs because the elevator was out of service. I had already gone down seven steps when I saw Professor Zizoloziz on the ground floor coming up. I continued descending at my usual pace, greeted the professor when we passed, and was surprised to see that when I still had four more steps to go, the professor had gone up the whole flight. "When I go down one step, he goes up two," I thought.

How many steps does the staircase have?

8. What Month—I

A month begins on a Friday and ends on a Friday, too. What month is it?

9. What Month—II

The result of adding the date of the last Monday of last month and the date of the first Thursday of next month is 38. If both dates are of the same year, what is the current month?

10. Eve's Enigma

After heaven, the earth, the grass, and all the animals were created, the snake, who was very smart, decided to make its own contribution.

It decided to lie every Tuesday, Thursday, and Saturday. For the other days of the week, it told the truth.

"Eve, dear Eve, why don't you try an apple?" the snake suggested.

"But I am not allowed to!" said Eve.

"Oh, no!" said the snake. "You can eat it today since it is Saturday and God is resting."

"No, not today," said Eve, "Maybe tomorrow."

"Tomorrow is Wednesday and it will be too late," insisted the snake.

This is how the snake tricked Eve.

What day of the week did this conversation take place?

11. Soccer Scores—I

A soccer tournament has just ended. Five teams participated and each one played once against each of the other teams. The winner of a match received 2 points, the losing team 0 points, and each team received 1 point for a tie.

The final results were:
Lions   6 points
Tigers   5 points
Bears   3 points
Orioles   1 point

We are missing one team, the Eagles. What was their point total?

12. Soccer Scores—II

In a three-team tournament, each team played once against each of the two other teams. Each team scored one goal.

The final results were:
Lions   3 points
Tigers   2 points
Bears   1 point

What was the score in each match?

13. What Time Is It—I

I'm looking at my watch. From this moment on, the hour hand will take exactly twice as long as the minute hand to reach the number six. What time is it?

14. What Time Is It—II

I'm looking at my watch. From this moment on, the hour hand will take exactly three times longer than the minute hand to reach the number six. What time is it?

15. What Time Is It—III

I'm looking at my watch. The hour hand is on one mark and the minute hand is on the next one. (By marks, we mean minute marks.) What time is it?

16. What Time Is It—IV

I'm looking at my watch. The hour hand is on one mark and the minute hand is on the previous one. (By marks, we mean minute marks.) What time is it?

17. Prohibited Connection

Using the numbers 1, 2, 3, 4, 5, and 6, put each of them in a circle. There is only one condition. The circles connected by a line cannot have consecutive numbers. For example, 4 cannot be connected with 3 or 5.

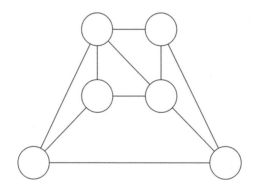

18. Concentric

The big square has an area of 60 square inches. Is there a fast way to figure out what the area of the small square is?

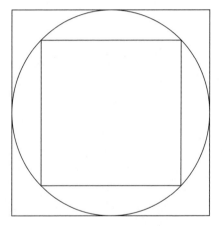

19. John Cash

John Cash saw his face on a poster nailed to a tree. As he approached, he saw "WANTED, DEAD OR ALIVE." Under his picture, it read "REWARD: ___ DOLLARS."

There was a three-digit figure on the poster. John drew his Colt and shot at the first number (in the hundreds column).

He had just reduced the price on his head by five times.

"Good Lord!" said the doctor's daughter, who was sitting on the other side of the tree doing her math homework.

John blushed, and shot again at another number (in the tens column).

He had just reduced the price on his head by another five times.

"Nice shooting!" said the young girl.

"Thank you, miss," said John. He spurred his horse and never returned.

What was the initial reward offered on John's head?

20. Russian Roulette

Russian roulette was created by Count Ugo Lombardo Fiumiccino, who successfully died during his first presentation of it.

He placed six jars on a shelf, as in the drawing on the next page. After staring at them, he closed his eyes and told his friend to fill them up with the ingredients, making sure that each jar contained an ingredient other than the one shown on its label.

When she was finished, the count asked:

"Dear Petrushka, would you be so kind as to tell me where the salt is?"

"Under the jar containing snuff," answered Petrushka.

"My dear friend, would you tell me where the sugar is?" he asked.

"Immediately to the right of the jar containing coffee," she answered.

Ugo Lombardo Fiumiccino, confirming his desire to commit suicide, reached immediately for the jar containing arsenic.

Where is the arsenic?

21. New Race

Two cars start traveling from two different points and in opposite directions in a circuit race at a constant speed. The cars cross for the first time at point A. The second time is at point B. The third time is at point C, and the fourth one is again at point A.

How much faster is one car going than the other?

22. Nice Discounts

A bookstore has a nice discount policy. If you buy a $20 book today, you get a 2% discount on your next purchase. If you buy a $15 book, you get a 1.5% discount on your next purchase. If you have to buy three books that cost $10, $20, and $30, you could buy the $30 book today, the $10 tomorrow (on which you'll get a 3% discount), and the $20 book the following day (on which you'll get a 1% discount). Or you could buy the $30 book and the $20 book today, and the $10 book tomorrow (with a 5% discount).

What is the cheapest way to buy five books priced at $10, $20, $30, $40, and $50?

23. The Calculator Keys

Several times Professor Zizoloziz mentioned that he feels uncomfortable looking at his pocket calculator. Yesterday, he was elated because he had found the reason why. The layout of the keys from 1 to 9 and the "minus" and "equal" signs look like they are doing subtraction. It's an incorrect one however, because 789 minus 456 does not equal 123. Zizoloziz thought of changing the numbers to achieve a correct equation. He changed 7 with 3, then 3 with 4, and 9 with 6, resulting in 486 − 359 = 127. He made only three changes to achieve this.

Using the keypad below as a reference, can you obtain a correctly subtracted number with only two changes?

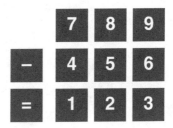

24. Enigmatic Fares

Professor Zizoloziz always adds the five digits on a bus transfer. Yesterday, he rode route 62 with a friend. As soon as he got the tickets, which were consecutively numbered, he added the numbers on them and then told his friend that the sum of all ten digits was exactly 62. His logical friend asked him if the sum of the numbers on either of the tickets was by any chance 35. Professor Zizoloziz answered and his friend then knew the numbers on the bus tickets.

What were the numbers on the two bus tickets?

25. Horoscope

An indiscreet young man asks his beautiful mathematics teacher her age. She responds, "Today's date is my age, although before this week is over there will be another day with a date one fifth of the new age that I will be."

What is the teacher's sign of the zodiac?

26. Strangers in the Night

The midnight train is coming down the Strujen-Bajen mountains. Art Farnanski seems to be dozing off in his seat.

Someone knows that this is not true.

At the station, all the passengers get off the train, except one. The conductor comes and taps him on the shoulder to let him know they have arrived. Art Farnanski does not answer. He is dead.

"His heart?" asks commander Abrojos, looking at the dead body.

"Strychnine," answers the forensic doctor.

Hours later, the four people that had shared the train compartment with the dead man are at the police station.

The man in the dark suit:
"I'm innocent. The blonde woman was talking to Farnanski."

The blonde woman:
"I'm innocent. I did not speak to Farnanski."

The man in the light suit:
"I'm innocent. The brunette woman killed him."

The brunette woman:

"I'm innocent. One of the men killed him."

That same morning, while he is serving him coffee, the waiter at the Petit Piccolo asks commander Abrojos:

"This is an easy case for you, isn't it?"

"Yes," answers the commander. "Four true statements and four false ones. Easy as pie."

Who killed Farnanski? (Only one person is guilty.)

27. The Foreigners and the Menu

A particular inn always offers the same nine dishes on its dinner menu: A, B, C, D, E, F, G, H, and I.

Five foreigners arrive. Nobody tells them which dish corresponds to each letter and so they each select one letter without knowing what they will eat.

The innkeeper arrives with the five dishes ordered and puts them in the center of the table so that they can decide who eats what.

This goes on for two more nights.

The foreigners, who are professors of logic, are able to deduce by the dishes they ordered which letter represents what dish.

What could have been the dishes ordered each of the three nights?

28. Monte Carlo

The famous playboy Hystrix Tardigradus explained to a beautiful woman his system for playing roulette:

"In each round, I always bet half of the money I have at the time on red. Yesterday, I counted and I had won as many rounds as I had lost."

Over the course of the night, did Hystrix win, lose, or break even?

29. The Harem

The story goes that the harem of the Great Tamerlan was protected by a door with many locks. A vizier and four slaves were in charge of guarding this door.

Knowledgeable of the weaknesses of men, the Great Tamerlan had distributed the keys in such a way that the vizier could only open the door if he was with any one of the slaves, and the slaves could only open it if three of them worked together.

How many locks did the door have?

30. The Dividing End

My ID number is quite remarkable. It's a nine-digit number with each of the digits from 1 to 9 appearing once. The whole number is divisible by 9. If you remove the rightmost digit, the remaining eight-digit number is divisible by 8. Removing the next rightmost digit leaves a seven-digit number that is divisible by 7. This property continues all the way down to one digit. What is my ID number?

31. A Warm Farewell

At a train station, the Porter family is saying good-bye to the Robinson family. We don't know who is leaving and who is staying.

Each of the members of the Porter family says farewell to each of the members of the Robinson family. To say good-bye, two men shake hands, and both a man and a woman and two women kiss once on the cheek.

An eyewitness to the event counts 21 handshakes and 34 kisses.

How many men and how many women are saying good-bye?

32. Added Corners

Using the numbers from 1 to 8, place one in each shape with one condition: The number in each square has to be the sum of its two neighboring circles.

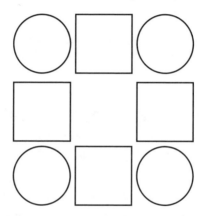

33. Logic Apples

Four perfect logicians, who all knew each other from being members of the Perfect Logicians' Club, sat around a table that had a dish with 11 apples in it. The chat was intense, and they ended up eating all the apples. Everybody had at least one apple, and everyone knew that fact, and each logician knew the number of apples that he ate. They didn't know how many apples each of the others ate, though. They agreed to ask only questions that they didn't know the answers to:

Alonso: Did you eat more apples than I did, Bertrand?

Bertrand: I don't know. Did you, George, eat more apples than I did?

George: I don't know.

Kurt: Aha!

Kurt figured out how many apples each person ate. Can you do the same?

34. The Island and the Englishmen

On a deserted island (except for a small group of Englishmen) there are four clubs.

The membership lists reveal that:

a) Each Englishman is a member of two clubs.

b) Every set of two clubs has only one member in common.

How many Englishmen are there on the island?

35. Rectangles

The vertical rectangle (solid line) has an area of 40 square inches.

Find out in a quick way the area of the inclined rectangle (dotted line).

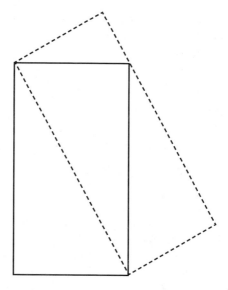

36. On the Route of Marco Polo

On his way east, Marco Polo passed five little villages along a straight road. At each village a road sign points to one of the other four villages. Below are the five signs, in no particular order. Can you add the corresponding arrows to the four signs that have lost them? (The five signs are all on the same side of the road.)

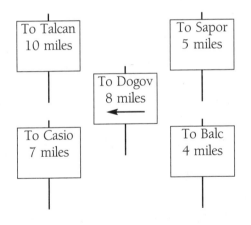

37. Touching Squares

Shown here are three squares on a table with each one touching the other two squares. If you want to place squares so that each square touches exactly three other squares (not counting corner-to-corner or corner-to-side contact), how many squares do you need? All squares must lie on the table surface.

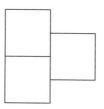

38. Blood and Sand

"You are the killer!" declared Commissioner Abrojos. His assistant, Inspector Begonias, slanted his eyes and looked around. They were alone in the room.

"I don't understand," he said.

"You are the killer!" the commissioner repeated adamantly.

Here is the story:

Yesterday, responding to a phone call, Inspector Begonias visited the mansion of millionaire Lincoln Dustin at around 7 P.M. The millionaire was dead in his office. There were blood stains on the carpet around the desk. Begonias inspected the place. He questioned the butler, who told him that Lincoln Dustin always led a perfectly ordered life. Every day, at noon, Mr. Dustin started the hourglass, the one that was now next to his dead body. At exactly midnight, the hourglass finished and Lincoln Dustin would go to sleep.

Begonias thought this was all very interesting, but not so useful for his investigation. That same night, the butler's call woke him up.

"Inspector!" cried the butler, "The hourglass did not finish at midnight, but at 3 A.M.!"

Begonias told all of this to Commissioner Abrojos.

"Let's suppose," said the commissioner, "that Mr. Dustin was able to turn the hourglass to leave us a clue as to the time of the crime."

Begonias nodded.

"In that case," continued the commissioner, "you told me that you had gone to the mansion around 7 P.M., which makes me think that you are the killer."

This is how they reached the conversation at the beginning of our puzzle.

Begonias could not believe it.

"I never thought," he said sadly, "that you would do this to me."

"Come on, Begonias, aren't you going to try to find an excuse?"

The inspector thought for a moment, going over the events of the previous day.

"The hourglass!" he cried. "I remember now. When I inspected the room I saw that the hourglass was on a handwritten note."

"Do you mean that the victim wrote the name of the killer? I don't believe that."

"Not at all!" said Begonias. "I wanted to read the note, so I lifted the hourglass and then I must have turned it upside down by mistake."

"What time was it then?"

"7 P.M."

"My dear friend, this clears you as a suspect!" said the commissioner.

Suppose that Mr. Dustin was able to invert the hourglass before dying. At what time did he die? Why did the commissioner consider Begonias as a suspect?

39. Equal Vision

Each watchman looks in all directions (horizontal, vertical, and diagonal). On the left board, each watchman has five vacant cells under his gaze. (A watchman can see beyond another watchman.) On the right, each watchman can see six empty cells. What's the maximum number of watchmen that can be placed so that each sees seven empty cells?

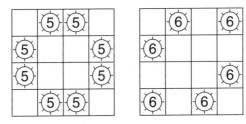

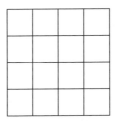

40. Mister Digit Face

Place each of the digits 1 to 9, one digit per blank, so that the product of the two eyes equals the number above the head, and the product of each eye and mouth equals the number on the respective side of the face.

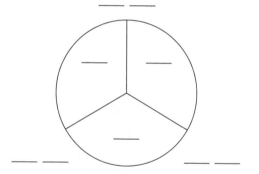

41. Digit Tree

Using each digit from 1 to 9 once, make seven numbers so that each number is equal to the sum of the numbers in the circles that are connected to it from below. (The numbers can be more than one digit.) There are two slightly different answers.

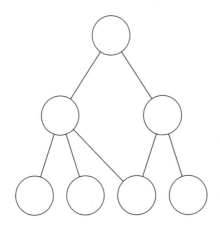

42. Segments

Place the digits 1 to 9 (using each digit once, one digit per box) so that:

• the boxes containing the 1 and 2 and all the ones between them add up to 12,

• the boxes containing the 2 and 3 and all the ones between them add up to 23,

• the boxes containing the 3 and 4 and all the ones between them add up to 34,

• the boxes containing the 4 and 5 and all the ones between them add up to 45.

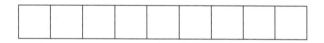

43. International Summit

At a recent international summit, five delegates (A, B, C, D, and E) participated. This is what we observed:

1. B and C spoke English, although when D joined them, they all changed to Spanish, the only common language among the three of them.

2. The only common language among A, B, and E was French.

3. The only common language between C and E was Italian.

4. Three delegates could speak Portuguese.

5. The most common language was Spanish.

6. One of the delegates spoke all five languages, another one spoke four, one spoke three, one spoke two, and the other spoke only one language.

What languages did each delegate speak?

44. Earthlings

August 2002.

The spaceship landed.

"Earth!" they shouted.

They knew that earthlings are divided into three groups: those who always tell the truth, those who always lie, and those who do both, alternating between true and false statements, starting with either.

"Let's go!" said the captain.

The aliens approached three earthlings, who each were from a different group, and asked, "Who won the last World Cup? Who came in second? Who came in third?"

One of them responded, "Zaire first. Uruguay second. Spain third."

Another one said, "Zaire first. Spain second. Uruguay third."

The third one said, "Uruguay first. Spain second. Zaire third."

The aliens returned to their spaceship and flew back to where they came from.

Do you know which response was the true ranking in the World Cup?

Hints

Page	Hint		Page	Hint
87	S T		110	J T
88	F B		111	T F
89	S R		112	M D
90	N B		113	S D
91	F M		114	F B
92	P D		115	P S
93	F M		116	T P
94	M S		117	T B
95	C Y		118	F B
96	B F		119	T M
97	K M		120	H F
98	K R		121	H S
99	R E		122	R B
100	F N		123	D T
101	A C		124	S T
102	L R		125	L Z
103	P P		126	P S
104	R W		127	R D
105	T M		128	F C
106	B S		129	L S
107	M D		130	A C
108	W S		131	B T
109	G B		132	L T

The first letter is the code letter; the second is the letter the code letter represents.

1 J represents G
2 H represents F
3 S represents G
4 I represents V
5 T represents V
6 S represents M
7 K represents R
8 T represents N
9 M represents V
10 W represents M
11 M represents N
12 A represents F
13 K represents R
14 B represents M
15 C represents W
16 F represents C
17 M represents W
18 U represents G
19 E represents M
20 V represents E
21 Z represents G
22 O represents N
23 S represents Y
24 H represents Y
25 A represents D
26 L represents M
27 E represents Y
28 Z represents B
29 A represents U
30 D represents B
31 R represents N
32 Z represents C
33 H represents O
34 M represents O
35 G represents H
36 D represents R
37 F represents H
38 R represents S
39 J represents T
40 C represents T
41 Z represents C
42 B represents N
43 X represents D
44 W represents C
45 I represents B
46 I represents L

47 O represents W
48 X represents D
49 W represents E
50 U represents O
51 V represents M
52 L represents U
53 O represents L
54 M represents T
55 R represents W
56 Z represents M
57 G represents S
58 O represents S
59 I represents U
60 X represents D
61 I represents D
62 T represents V
63 O represents W
64 L represents T

65 D represents Y
66 G represents B
67 S represents Y
68 E represents T
69 P represents N
70 D represents I
71 S represents H
72 M represents H
73 C represents N
74 J represents R
75 N represents O
76 D represents P
77 H represents R
78 Y represents F
79 V represents C
80 T represents P
81 B represents I
82 A represents P

1 Black's first move doesn't look so good.

2 Positioning plays an important role.

3 Black's first move looks almost suicidal.

4 White cuts off Black's options.

5 Sacrifice, sacrifice, sacrifice.

6 He offers White two opportunities to jump instead of one.

7 There's a spectacular setup situation that sets up the victory.

8 Sacrifice plays pave the way.

9 This will take a lot of foresight and planning.

10 Black starts with a very unlikely-looking sacrifice.

11 31 to 27 would give Black a draw after he went from 18 to 22.

12 Black forgoes the obvious crowning opportunity on his first move.

13 White forces Black into an extremely vulnerable position.

14 Black forces White into an untenable position for a big multiple capture.

15 It's a series of sacrifices, combinations, and positioning in four plays.

16 Don't start by going from 25 to 29 for a second king.

17 Sacrifice moves are the key.

18 A view from the other end of the board might help.

19 It doesn't start with a sacrifice, but it is a forcing move.

20 Pre-planning and perfect timing earn Black a sextuple jump for the win.

21 Black forgoes the opportunity to save his man on 9.

22 Black doesn't move into his king row until it will do the most good.

23 Black has to give up a lot to get a lot back (including the win).

24 It must be done right now from this position.

25 Look at this from White's end of the board.

26 Black forces White into a very vulnerable position.

27 Think big and bold!

28 Think diagonally.

29 It's now or never for White.

30 The three plays are all forcing and must be done immediately.

31 White maneuvers Black into an inescapable trap.

32 Position and whose turn it is to go are often deciding factors.

33 Black doesn't go right in for a king.

Answers

Ages of Reason

Aunt Pearl is 64 years old (LXIV) and her daughter is 46 (XLVI). The numbers 66 (LXVI) and 44 (XLIV) can also be made from the same symbols.

Animal Strength

The frogs will win the third tug of war. Two turtles will tie with four frogs.

Berry Impressive

There will be 34 strawberries at the beginning of November. The number of berries each month is the famous Fibonacci sequence (1, 1, 2, 3, 5, 8, ...), where each number is the sum of the previous two.

Black and White

1. You have two white cards.
2. You have one white card and one black card. (If you had two black cards, A would know what he had on the second round, because if he had two of the same card, one of you would have seen four of one color and known you had two of the other color.)

Blind Alleys

They started in Redland.

Block Party

She took the "CUBE ROUTE."

Fishing for Words

The proverb reads, "The fish dies because he opens his mouth."

Fishing Lines

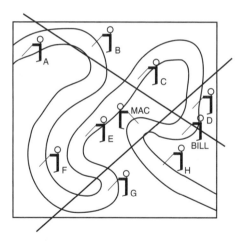

For Your Thoughts

1. A
2. C

Fraction Words

A. Florida (fl + or + ida)
B. piano (pi + an + o)

Game Plan

A: Player X wins; B: Player X wins (X plays above O first, then no matter where O plays, X can either win on the next turn or take the lowest empty right-hand box and win on the following turn).

A Good Egg

1. T; 2. W; 3. E; 4. L; 5. V; 6. E. An ostrich egg equals about 24 hen's eggs, or 12 omelets.

Got Class?

This class schedule will work: Biology, European history, Genetics, Shakespeare, and Statistics.

Graphic Language

Because seven eight nine ("seven ate nine").

Hairy Tales

1. Rapunzel was trapped for 200 years.
2. Rip Van Winkle's beard should have been 10 feet long.

Keep the Faith

Old Faithful's next eruption will be at 4:50 P.M. The formula used to figure out the time until the next eruption is 4D + 30 minutes, where D is the duration of the last eruption.

Losing Track

Deb cheated. The answers are: 1. bison; 2. caribou; 3. deer; 4. moose; 5. mountain goat.

Match Boxes

Only piece e will not form a box.

Mind Boggler

The numbers ONE through TEN can be spelled by moving from letter to adjacent letter. THREE is the only number that cannot be spelled (without using the same E two times in a row).

Mirror Images

Figures four and seven are impossible with just one mirror.

Next in Line

Each item is spelled with all the letters from the one before, plus one: TEA, TAPE, PLEAT, and STAPLE. The next item in the sequence is PLANETS (a).

Paper Clip Flip

Number 1 is shorter than the original. Numbers 3 and 10 are longer than the original.

Produce Products

The equations are: $9 - 3 = 6$; $4 \times 2 = 8$; $1 + 4 = 5$; and $6 \div 3 = 2$. Therefore, the carrot is 7.

Sea or Soil?

The treasure is buried underwater.

Self Test

1. 8; 2. 6; 3. 4; 4. 1; 5. 9; 6. 7; 7. 5; 8. 3; 9. 2.

Slice of Life

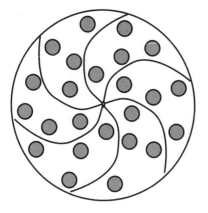

Technique-Color

Piece A should be orange.

Ten Gold Coins

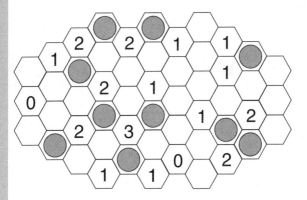

Theory of Relativity

You are Bernie.

Thirteen Candles

The candles form 50 triangles: 18 made by the six points around the edge; 18 using the full side of the two large triangles; 12 made of half of a full side; and 2 large triangles.

Three Hexes
Numbers three and seven are made with four hexagons.

12-Step Program
The output reads: BOOT UP.

Tying the Knot
She should start her subscription to *Brides* magazine. Ropes 1, 2, and 5 will form knots.

What's the Plan?
Object one fits the plan.

Winter Eyes
A–1; B–7; C–4.

Puzzle 1

ACROSS

1 W+IMPS
4 BOATS (acronym)
7 IN+SEx+PARABLE
8 K(IN)K+Y (*Y KK* rev.)
9 NO(V)EL
10 PROW+L
12 MALT+A
14 DE+MOS(THEN)ES
15 ELDER (2 defs.)
16 A+DEPT.

DOWN

1 WHISKy
2 M+IS IN FOR+ME+D
3 S(OP)PY
4 BAR+ON
5 AMBI(VAL)ENCE
6 S+WELL
10 P+ADRE (*read* anag.)
11 LA(S)ER (*real* rev.)
12 MEHT+A (*them* rev.)
13 A+SSET (all rev.)

Puzzle 2

ACROSS

4 ARe+BIT+RATES
6 PSIS (*size* hom.)
7 BIN+DER (all rev.)
8 RARE (acronym)
9 HA(N)G
12 CLOT+HE
14 IN+NS
15 MAN+ITO+BANS

DOWN

1 A+BUS+ER
2 PA(W)N
3 DETER+GENTS
4 A+US+TRA+LIAN (*nail art* rev.)
5 TUBS (anag.)
10 A(NI)MAL (all rev.)
11 K+ENO (all rev.)
13 TAIL (*tale* hom.)

Puzzle 3

ACROSS

1 SA(TIN)Y
5 IF(F)Y (*FYI* anag.)
7 J+I'VE
8 N(EVAD)A (*Dave* rev.)
9 RUMP+US
10 SEE'D (pun)
11 I+CON
13 QUINCE (2 defs.)
15 ATTILA (hidden)
16 A+V(O)W
17 SH(O)E
18 FLE+XES (all rev.)

DOWN

2 ADIE+U (*idea* anag.)
3 IN+EX+PENSIVE
4 YANKS (2 defs.)
5 IN(caVE)STIGATE
6 FUDGE (2 defs.)
12 CAT+CH
13 QUArt+FF
14 CLOSE (2 defs.)

Puzzle 4

ACROSS

1 L+ACE
3 FORMER (2 defs.)
7 G(R)UFF
9 T(OX)IC
10 SU(BAT)OMI+C
12 BE(GIN)NING
16 CIVIC (palindrome)
17 SO+USA
18 SOLE+I+L
19 A+KINg

DOWN

1 LOG+O
2 C(O)UPS
4 OUTS+TRIPS (*to us* anag.)
5 MA+XIM (*mix* rev.)
6 R+O+COCO
8 FIB+ON+A+CCI (*I.C.C.* rev.)
11 A+B(AC)US
13 GAVE+L
14 G+LUCK
15 DAW+N (*wad* rev.)

Puzzle 5

ACROSS

1 ON+C(E)OVER
7 AVID (rev.)
8 LASTED (anag.)
9 A+GREED
10 YET+I
11 S(T)UB
13 BU(SILver)Y
15 WORSEN (anag.)
16 W H I P (pun)
17 MI+SPRINT

DOWN

2 N(A+VIG)ATION
3 END(U)E (*need* anag.)
4 VALID (anag.)
5 RI+SKY
6 SEP(TILL+IO)N (*ESPN* anag.)
12 BO(S)OM
13 B(ON)US
14 S+EWER

Puzzle 6

ACROSS

4 ARCHFIENDS (anag.)
7 FLOW-ER (pun)
8 DEN+Y
9 APE+X
11 FRO+G
13 Z+INCh
14 HURR(A)Y
16 PER+SUA(SI)VE

DOWN

1 PAL+LIAT+I'VE (*tail* rev.)
2 S+COW
3 TENDER (2 defs.)
5 F(U)RY
6 DENI(GR)ATED (*detained* rev.)
10 EXCISE (2 defs.)
12 RHEA (hidden)
15 RUINg

Puzzle 7

ACROSS

1 FRAC(A)S (all rev.)
5 J+IN+X
7 F(LAPP)ABLE
8 IS IS (pun)
9 LEE+R
11 AFAR (hidden)
13 SO+UP
15 ST(R)APLE+SS
16 GYMS (acronym)
17 DA(SHE)D

DOWN

2 REFUSE (2 defs.)
3 C(OATS)O+FARMS
4 SE(P)AL
5 JO(BLESS)NES'S
6 NEED (knead hom.)
10 PURS(U)E
12 RA(P)ID
14 E(SP)Y (all rev.)

Puzzle 8

ACROSS

1 CONVERGE (anag.)
7 DROL+L (lord rev.)
8 BAR(G)E
9 LIEDE(TECTO)R (octet anag.)
11 CAP+ITAL(C+IT)Y
16 TRAC+K (cart rev.)
17 VI+AND (IV rev.)
18 HONOREES (anag.)

DOWN

2 OZ+ONE
3 V+A(L)VE
4 RUB(L)E
5 rEGRET
6 BE+TRAYED (trade hom.)
7 D(ELI+C)ATE
10 TEA (odd letters)
12 P+EACH
13 TO+KEN
14 cLEVER
15 I+RATE

Puzzle 9

ACROSS

1 PO(U)ND
4 PU+PIL (all rev.)
7 ODIST (hidden)
8 NIX+ON
9 OR(SON)WELL+E+S
10 CO(ME-TOO)RDER
14 ZO(RR)O
15 I(NEP)T (*pen* rev.)
16 NEE(D)S (all rev.)
17 MOO+D+Y

DOWN

1 PROM+O
2 U(N+IT)S
3 D(ET)ONATIONS
4 PANDEMONIUM (anag.)
5 PI+XEL (*lex* rev.)
6 LIN+KS (*nil* rev.)
10 COZEN (*cousin* hom.)
11 MER(G)E
12 DIE+GO
13 R+ATTY

Puzzle 10

ACROSS

1 APOSTROPHE (anag.)
8 A+GAT+E
9 ALOES (even letters)
10 C,A,K,E
11 EDIS+ON (*side* rev.)
13 SI(MIA)N
15 OH(I)O
18 I(F+NO)T
19 REVUE (hidden rev.)
20 KNOWITALLS (anag.)

DOWN

2 P+RANK
3 S(U)EZ
4 R(WAND)+A
5 P+IOUS
6 EISENHOWER (anag.)
7 MAT+CH(ST)ICK
12 MAITAI (*might I* hom.)
14 MANGO (anag.)
16 sHOVEL
17 AREnA

Puzzle 11

ACROSS

1 GERMany
4 BA(M)BOOn
7 DISH+ARM(ON)Y
8 P+ADDLE
9 C+APE
10 JO'S+H
12 POW(D)ER
14 PR(OVEN)ANCE
15 ODES+SAw
16 AU+T+O

DOWN

2 EN+DE(A)VOURED
3 M(USE)D
4 B(LAD)E
5 MIMI+C
6 OM+NI+PRESENT (*in MO* rev.)
11 H(I'VE)S
12 P AND A
13 WONK+A (*know* rev.)

Puzzle 12

ACROSS

1 MAD+AMS
7 OF FISH
8 WEN+TUP (all rev.)
9 H(OLD)IT
10 CAME+RAW+OMEN
14 BHUTTO (anag.)
15 RAV(IN)E
16 A+SHORE
17 NAR+ROW (*ran* rev.)

DOWN

2 ALE+XI+A
3 AC+TONE
4 SO(PHIAL+ORE)N
5 WISDOM (hidden)
6 WH(IT)EN
10 CO+BRAS
11 M+OUT+H...Y
12 O+LIVER
13 EVENSO (hidden)

Puzzle 13

ACROSS

1 gEN(TRACT)E
6 RO(B)OTS
7 L+AID
8 M(AX)I (*I'm* rev.)
9 S+IMPLY
10 CA(C)T+US
13 RED+O
15 D(IS)C
16 UR(CHI)N
17 PIGLAT(I)N (*plating* anag.)

DOWN

1 E+GOT+ISTICAL (*italics* anag.)
2 T+ASKS
3 AL(LAMER)I+CAN
4 T+WILL
5 GO+YAle
11 ALIBI (hidden)
12 S(QUA)T
14 DA(I)'S

Puzzle 14

ACROSS

4 RECON+CILER (*relic* rev.)
7 SOW+HAT
8 GAG+A
9 N(Y)ET
11 STEM (rev.)
13 C(H)AT
14 OW(N)ING
16 CHAR(DONNA)Y

DOWN

1 HERO(INCH)IC
2 NOS+H (all rev.)
3 PLIGHT (2 defs.)
5 CUTS (odd letters)
6 R(EG+IM)ENTAL
10 ENTRAP (anag.)
12 WOO+D
15 NIN+E

Puzzle 15

ACROSS

1 SHOULDer
5 WE+A+K
7 AF+FI+LIATED (*detail if* rev.)
8 HYDE (*hied* hom.)
9 L(ARE)DO (*old* anag.)
10 C(LOSE)D
13 OO+PS
15 BE+LAB+ART+OK
16 NA(V)Y
17 AGEISM (anag.)

DOWN

2 HE(F)TY (*they* anag.)
3 UN(I'VE)R+SALLY (*run* anag.)
4 DR+ILL
5 WATERCOURSE (anag.)
6 A(DDE)D
11 LIBYA (hid. rev.)
12 DEBRA (anag.)
14 PRO+M'S

Puzzle 16

ACROSS

1 BOLT (2 defs.)
3 S+W+EDEN
7 GAS+P
8 F+RIGHT
10 F(O+OTB)ALL
13 PIN(NACL)E
16 E(QUIT)Y (*ye* rev.)
17 M+IN+I
18 MO(THE)+R
19 EG+G'S

DOWN

1 BU(GO)FF
2 LESS+ON
4 WARP+LANE
5 DO(G)S (*sod* rev.)
6 NOT+E
9 A+B'S+IN+THE
11 A+CHIN+G
12 G(E)NIUS (*suing* rev.)
14 S'EAM (rev.)
15 BUS+T

Puzzle 17

ACROSS

1 D(wEB)UG
4 TUCKS (*tux* hom.)
7 FITFO+RAKING (*it off* anag.)
8 YELL OW
9 KI(L)N
11 M(A)R. X
12 J+ARGON
15 A(SYOUL)-I+KEIT (*kite, lousy* anags.)
16 T(jULy)IP
17 C(LOT)H

DOWN

1 DA(FF)Y
2 BATTLEROYAL (anag. – *G*)
3 GO(O)-GO+L
4 TEAR (anag.)
5 CEILINGZERO (anag. – *f*)
6 SAGA+N
10 MA+NIAC (*Cain* rev.)
11 ME+ANT
13 N+OT(C)H (*hot* anag.)
14 GUM+Pin

Puzzle 18

ACROSS

4 MA(RVALBE)RT (*verbal* anag.)
7 F+LEA
8 S(QUE)+AK
9 GA(E)L
10 LONG (2 defs.)
13 T+AND+EM (*me* rev.)
15 ACTS (anag.)
16 C(HET)ATKINS (*the* anag.)

DOWN

1 A(VIA)TE
2 MEN+oUt
3 STRAIGHTEN (anag.)
5 ALL(EG)IANCE
6 L(IS)P
11 OZ+ARKS
12 YM+CA (*my* rev.)
14 DREW (2 defs.)

Puzzle 19

ACROSS

1 OBOE ([r]owboa[t] hom.)
4 S+UPPER
7 ARM+AN+I
8 TI+FF (*it* rev.)
9 LIME (anag.)
10 MAY+HEM
11 BU(SHE)S
14 TUTU (*too-too* hom.)
15 T+A+PE
16 O+NET+WO
17 REMARK (rev.)
18 AWRY (*a rye* hom.)

DOWN

2 B+ARBIT(U)RATE
3 ER(A)SE
4 SEIS+M
5 P+I+THY
6 E+IF+FELT+OWER (*wore* anag.)
12 H(YEN)A
13 S+HOOK
14 THE+TA

Puzzle 20

ACROSS

1 C(H)OPPING
6 ALLY (2 defs.)
7 M+A(T)ERIAL
9 B(L)UFF
12 DIR+TFLOOR (*rid* rev., or *loft* anag.)
13 ELLINGTON (move *t* in *telling on*)
15 NIS+EI (all rev.)
17 DO+M(IN)ATE
18 F+I DO
19 N+AGGIES+T

DOWN

1 CO+MEDIAN
2 OUTCRIES (anag.)
3 PORTFOLI+O (*for pilot* anag.)
4 GALLOn
5 CLEFt
8 AB+OUNDING (*undoing* anag.)
10 sURE+THANE
11 FA+IN+TEST
14 wimbLEDON
16 I+RIS (*sir* rev.)

Page	Answer	Page	Answer
87	Sleepy tepee	110	Jolly trolley
88	Fat bat	111	Thin Finn
89	Space race	112	Mice dice
90	Noah's boas	113	Smelly deli
91	Fender mender	114	Funny bunny
92	Poodle's doodles	115	Pickup stickup
93	Funky monkey	116	Toto photo
94	Miner shiner	117	Tall ball
95	Cranky Yankee	118	Full bull
96	Beast feast	119	Tragic magic
97	Kitten's mittens	120	Height fright
98	King's rings	121	Huge Scrooge
99	Regal eagle	122	Rooster booster
100	Fun nun	123	Damp tramp
101	Ape cape	124	Stone throne
102	Laser razor	125	Libra zebra
103	Phony pony	126	Pope scope
104	Rich witch	127	Ranger danger
105	Tut mutt	128	Fox clocks
106	Brave shave	129	Leopard shepherd
107	Mummy dummy	130	Apple chapel
108	Wall scrawl	131	Beef thief
109	Goat boat	132	Limber timber

INTRODUCTION: If at first you don't succeed, try, try again.

1 The brain is a wonderful organ; it starts the minute you get up in the morning and does not stop until you get to the office. —Robert Frost

2 There are two times in a man's life when he should not speculate: when he can't afford it, and when he can. —Mark Twain

3 Why is it when we talk to God, we're said to be praying, but when God talks to us, we're schizophrenic? —Lily Tomlin

4 The great thing about the movies is you're giving people little tiny pieces of time that they never forget. —Jimmy Stewart

5 Everywhere I go I'm asked if I think the university stifles writers. My opinion is that they don't stifle enough of them. —Flannery O'Connor

6 We didn't all come over on the same ship, but we're all in the same boat. —Bernard Baruch

7 It took me seventeen years to get three thousand hits in baseball. I did it in one afternoon on the golf course. —Hank Aaron

8 There's no trick to being a humorist when you have the whole government working for you.
—Will Rogers

9 I often have long conversations with myself, and I am so clever that sometimes I don't understand a single word I am saying. —Oscar Wilde

10 Nearly all men can stand adversity, but if you want to test a man's character, give him power.
—Abraham Lincoln

11 Sometimes it's necessary to go a long distance out of the way in order to come back a short distance correctly. —Edward Albee

12 We owe a lot to Thomas Edison. If it weren't for him, we'd be watching television by candlelight.
—Milton Berle

13 Never tell people how to do things. Tell them what to do and they will surprise you with their ingenuity. —George Patton

14 Too many people expect wonders from democracy, when the most wonderful thing of all is just having it. —Walter Winchell

15 A celebrity is someone who works hard all his life to become well-known, and then wears dark glasses to avoid being recognized. —Fred Allen

16 The way to catch a knuckleball is to wait until the ball stops rolling and then pick it up. —Bob Uecker

17 There are two insults no human being will endure: that he has no sense of humor, and that he has never known trouble. —Sinclair Lewis

18 You got to be careful if you don't know where you're going, because you might not get there. —Yogi Berra

19 It took me fifteen years to discover I had no talent for writing, but I couldn't give it up because by that time I was too famous.   —Robert Benchley

20 You may be disappointed if you fail, but you are doomed if you don't try.   —Beverly Sills

21 The only thing I regret about my past is the length of it. If I had to live my life again, I'd make the same mistakes, only sooner.   —Tallulah Bankhead

22 I maintain that the phrase "a long poem" is simply a contradiction in terms.   —Edgar Allan Poe

23 People learn something every day, and a lot of times it's that what they learned the day before was wrong.   —Bill Vaughan

24 We've had trickle-down economics in the country for years now, and most of us aren't even damp yet.   —Molly Ivins

25 Do not the most moving moments of our lives find us all without words?   —Marcel Marceau

26 Middle age is the awkward period when Father Time starts catching up with Mother Nature.

—Harold Coffin

27 Getting divorced just because you don't love a man is almost as silly as getting married just because you do.

—Zsa Zsa Gabor

28 Never lend books, for no one ever returns them; the only books I have in my library are books that other folk have lent me.

—Anatole France

29 The trouble with equality is that we only desire it with our superiors.

—Henry Becque

30 I don't think of all the misery but of all the beauty that still remains.

—Anne Frank

31 There are two things that will be believed of any man whatsoever, and one of them is that he has taken to drink.

—Booth Tarkington

32 A vegetarian is somebody who won't eat anything that can have children.

—David Brenner

33 You can live a lifetime and, at the end of it, know more about other people than you know about yourself.   —Beryl Markham

34 Human beings are the only creatures on Earth that allow their children to come back home.
                                            —Bill Cosby

35 I never could understand how two men can write a book together; to me that's like three people getting together to have a baby.   —Evelyn Waugh

36 The trouble with life in the fast lane is that you get to the other end in an awful hurry.
                                            —John Jensen

37 One doesn't discover new lands without consenting to lose sight of the shore for a very long time.   —André Gide

38 A study of economics usually reveals that the best time to buy anything is last year. —Marty Allen

39 Man's mind stretched to a new idea never goes back to its original dimensions.
                              —Oliver Wendell Holmes

40 If the public likes you, you're good. Shakespeare was a common, down-to-earth writer in his day.
—Mickey Spillane

41 Life is easier than you'd think; all that is necessary is to accept the impossible, do without the indispensable, and bear the intolerable.
—Kathleen Norris

42 I am only a public entertainer who has understood his time. —Pablo Picasso

43 Blessed is the man who, having nothing to say, abstains from giving wordy evidence of the fact.
—George Eliot

44 Politics is not a bad profession. If you succeed there are many rewards, if you disgrace yourself you can always write a book. —Ronald Reagan

45 The point of living, and of being an optimist, is to be foolish enough to believe the best is yet to come.
—Peter Ustinov

46 Character builds slowly, but it can be torn down with incredible swiftness. —Faith Baldwin

47 Experience is not what happens to you; it is what you do with what happens to you.

—Aldous Huxley

48 The easiest way to convince my kids that they don't really need something is to get it for them.

—Joan Collins

49 All I need to make a comedy is a park, a policeman, and a pretty girl.   —Charlie Chaplin

50 A man begins cutting his wisdom teeth the first time he bites off more than he can chew.

—Herb Caen

51 Personally, I think if a woman hasn't met the right man by the time she's twenty-four, she may be lucky.

—Deborah Kerr

52 I used to work in a fire hydrant factory. You couldn't park anywhere near the place.

—Steven Wright

53 There are two ways of spreading light: to be the candle or the mirror that reflects it.

—Edith Wharton

54 A bore is someone who persists in holding his own views after we have enlightened him with ours.

—Malcolm Forbes

55 The trouble with the profit system has always been that it is highly unprofitable to most people.

—E.B. White

56 One of the oldest human needs is having someone to wonder where you are when you don't come home at night. —Margaret Mead

57 The only thing that saves us from the bureaucracy is its inefficiency. —Eugene McCarthy

58 My father used to say that it was wicked to go fishing on Sunday. But he never said anything about draw poker. —Grover Cleveland

59 You can build a throne with bayonets, but you can't sit on it for long. —Boris Yeltsin

60 Some books are to be tasted, others to be swallowed, and some few to be chewed and digested. —Francis Bacon

61 Parents of young children should realize that few people will find their children as enchanting as they do. —Barbara Walters

62 Great events make me quiet and calm; it is only trifles that irritate my nerves. —Queen Victoria

63 He who cannot forgive others destroys the bridge over which he himself must pass. —George Herbert

64 Old age is like everything else. To make a success of it, you've got to start young. —Fred Astaire

65 Babies are always more trouble than you thought—and more wonderful. —Charles Osgood

66 The ad in the paper said "Big Sale. Last Week." Why advertise? I already missed it. They're just rubbing it in. —Yakov Smirnoff

67 It goes without saying that you should never have more children than you have car windows.
—Erma Bombeck

68 People who work sitting down get paid more than people who work standing up.   —Ogden Nash

69 If only one could have two lives: the first in which to make one's mistakes, and the second in which to profit by them.   —D.H. Lawrence

70 When people keep telling you that you can't do a thing, you kind of like to try it.
—Margaret Chase Smith

71 Washington appears to be filled with two kinds of politicians—those trying to get an investigation started, and those trying to get one stopped.
—Earl Wilson

72 Don't be humble. You're not that great.
—Golda Meir

73 The impersonal hand of government can never replace the helping hand of a neighbor.
—Hubert H. Humphrey

74 Trouble is a sieve through which we sift our acquaintances. Those too big to pass through are our friends. —Arlene Francis

75 This will remain the land of the free only so long as it is the home of the brave. —Elmer Davis

76 If you can keep your head when all about you are losing theirs, it's just possible you haven't grasped the situation. —Jean Kerr

77 The remarkable thing about Shakespeare is that he really is very good, in spite of all the people who say he is very good. —Robert Graves

78 A man's got to take a lot of punishment to write a really funny book. —Ernest Hemingway

79 You can easily judge the character of a man by how he treats those who can do nothing for him. —James D. Miles

80 I hate television. I hate it as much as peanuts. But I can't stop eating peanuts. —Orson Welles

81 The best and most beautiful things in the world cannot be seen or even touched. They must be felt with the heart. —Helen Keller

82 Why is propaganda so much more successful when it stirs up hatred than when it tries to stir up friendly feeling? —Bertrand Russell

1

A	I	D	A		A	L	A	M	O
D	R	O	P		P	A	L	I	N
L	A	I	T		P	L	A	T	E
I	N	N		L	E	A	S	E	S
B	I	G	D	E	A	L			
		A	M	R	A	D	I	O	
B	R	A	V	O	S		E	R	A
R	U	N	I	N		E	T	A	S
A	S	K	E	D		R	O	T	E
T	E	A	S	E		E	X	E	S

2

R	A	B	E		M	A	C	H	O
A	C	E	R		A	R	Y	A	N
S	T	E	R		S	A	B	L	E
T	O	R	O		A	L	E		
A	N	G	L	E	D		R	D	A
S	E	A		L	A	P	S	E	S
		R	A	P		A	P	E	S
N	A	D	I	A		N	A	P	E
E	D	E	N	S		I	C	E	R
T	O	N	T	O		C	E	N	T

3

W	O	K	S	■	T	S	A	R	S
A	N	E	W	■	O	P	R	A	H
G	E	R	E	■	N	A	D	I	R
S	A	R	A	H	■	R	O	S	E
■	■	■	T	A	P	E	R	E	D
S	L	I	P	S	U	P	■	■	■
T	A	R	A	■	B	A	N	J	O
E	L	A	N	D	■	R	E	A	P
M	A	N	T	A	■	T	A	K	E
S	W	I	S	S	■	S	P	E	D

4

D	E	B	S	■	I	M	P	E	L
E	D	I	T	■	M	A	O	R	I
L	I	A	R	■	P	R	O	M	O
E	N	L	A	C	E	■	P	A	N
S	A	Y	W	H	A	T	■	■	■
■	■	■	S	U	C	R	O	S	E
R	O	C	■	T	H	E	H	A	J
A	G	A	I	N	■	B	A	B	E
C	R	A	N	E	■	E	R	I	C
K	E	N	N	Y	■	K	E	N	T

5

C	A	P	R	I		S	L	E	W
A	L	L	E	N		C	O	M	E
B	L	E	A	K	H	O	U	S	E
B	U	D		Y	E	N			
E	D	G	E		N	E	W	T	S
D	E	E	M	S		S	H	U	T
			I	I	I		I	M	A
B	I	N	G	C	R	O	S	B	Y
O	V	E	R		A	N	K	L	E
B	Y	T	E		N	O	S	E	D

6

P	R	A	M		S	A	L	A	D
R	E	D	O		A	G	A	P	E
O	M	O	O		Y	I	P	E	S
B	A	R	N	O	W	L			
E	K	E		T	H	E	S	E	S
S	E	D	A	T	E		T	N	T
			C	O	N	B	R	I	O
H	O	H	U	M		R	I	S	K
A	N	I	T	A		I	D	L	E
W	O	M	E	N		G	E	E	S

7

C	H	A	D		D	E	F	A	T
L	A	N	E		O	C	A	L	A
O	L	D	S		C	O	M	I	X
D	O	Y	E	N			I	C	E
		W	R	E	S	T	L	E	R
S	K	A	T	E	K	E	Y		
W	A	R			A	C	R	E	S
A	S	H	E	N		H	O	L	E
P	H	O	T	O		N	O	S	E
S	A	L	A	D		O	M	A	N

8

L	E	S		D	O	T	E	L	L
E	L	Y		A	Z	A	L	E	A
T	I	N		B	A	K	I	N	G
O	H	O	S		R	E	S	T	S
N	U	D	N	I	K	S			
			I	M	S	O	R	R	Y
S	L	I	P	S		N	E	A	P
C	A	M	P	U	S		E	R	R
A	M	P	E	R	E		V	E	E
T	E	S	T	E	E		E	R	S

9

10

11

R	A	T		R	I	D	G	E	D
E	L	I		I	D	E	A	T	E
H	A	N	G	G	L	I	D	E	R
E	N	G	A	G	E				
M	O	L	L		S	P	E	C	S
S	N	E	E	R		E	V	A	N
				E	L	N	I	N	O
F	R	E	E	L	A	N	C	E	R
E	A	R	N	E	D		T	R	E
Z	Y	G	O	T	E		S	S	S

12

B	B	K	I	N	G		M	O	M
U	R	A	N	I	A		A	D	E
Y	E	L	P	E	D		N	I	N
S	W	E	L	L		O	N	U	S
			A	L	A	B	A	M	A
Z	I	P	C	O	D	E			
A	L	O	E		D	R	O	V	E
P	I	E		D	U	L	L	E	S
P	A	T		I	C	I	E	S	T
A	D	S		D	E	N	O	T	E

13

F	R	E	T		C	H	A	M	P
R	A	V	E		A	U	D	I	O
A	B	E	D		S	L	O	T	S
M	I	N	K		H	A	S	T	E
E	N	T	E	R	E	D			
			N	E	W	A	G	E	R
C	H	A	N	T			N	A	M	E
L	O	S	E	R		C	L	A	P
O	U	T	D	O		E	L	I	E
P	R	A	Y	S		R	O	L	L

14

C	O	P		G	A	S	C	A	P
O	H	O		A	T	H	O	M	E
P	A	P	E	R	T	O	W	E	L
E	R	I	N		H	E	S	S	E
S	A	N	D	R	A				
			A	T	O	D	D	S
S	O	L	T	I		N	O	R	A
T	H	E	O	D	Y	S	S	E	Y
E	N	T	R	E	E		E	S	E
P	O	S	E	R	S		S	S	R

15

16

17

18

19

```
N O M A D S ■ M E N
A R A B I A ■ O L E
P A L I N D R O M E
S L I T ■ D O L E D
■ ■ ■ B L E A R Y
S A T I R E ■ ■ ■
A G I L E ■ D A F T
W A L L A W A L L A
E V E ■ D E N I E D
R E D ■ S T A T E S
```

20

```
A B A T E D ■ J A G
D E R I D E ■ O W E
O R A N G E P E E L
B A R ■ E R E ■ ■ ■
E T A L ■ E L G A R
S E T I N ■ T O T O
■ ■ M O M ■ B R A
T H E B E A T L E S
R E V ■ L Y R I S T
A X E ■ S A I N T S
```

We hope that you've only had to check this section to verify your puzzle-solving prowess. But hardly anyone knows all the answers, so these solutions should provide intriguing insights into the strategy and tactics that will prove to be of special value in real checker games. All of these exercises should definitely increase your playing enjoyment and improve your winning record with the universally popular "granddaddy of board games."

1. Black startles White with 2 to 7 and White jumps in for a king from 11 to 2. Then Black goes from 9 to 13 so the new White monarch leaps from 2 to 9. Now, instead of taking the triple jump from 5 to 14 to 21 to 30 for a tie, Black jumps from 13 to 22. White must jump back from 25 to 18, giving White a triple leap from 5 to 14 to 23 to 32, where he obtains a king that will readily snare the White checker on 29 before it can reach the king row at the other end of the board. Well played!

2. First Black sacrifices 12 to 16 and White jumps from 19 to 12. Then Black gets a double jump by moving from 5 to 9 and leaping from 1 to 10 to 19 after White hops from 13 to 6. White has to capture from 23 to 16, providing Black's king on 30 with a jump to 23. Black's two kings are too much for White

to handle from his severely restricted position on the periphery of the board and he quickly goes down in flames.

3. Black gives White a king by moving from 3 to 7 and White jumps from 12 to 3. Then Black goes from 9 to 13 and the new White monarch jumps to 10, giving Black a double jump into his king row from 13 to 22 to 31. Now White has to leap from 15 to 8, which opens up a triple jump for Black from 6 to 15 to 22 to 29 for a gratifying win! Note: If White had taken the 15-to-8 jump on his second turn, the same series of subsequent jumps would have taken place with the same end result.

4. White sacrifices two of his kings by moving one from 18 to 22, and after Black jumps from 17 to 26, White moves his monarch on 19 to 24 so Black must leap from 20 to 27. Next White moves his last king from 15 to 10 and lets Black move his men up the board until they run out of moves, while he shuttles his king back and forth on squares 6 and 9 for a bizarre blocking victory.

5. White initiates a well-planned and well-timed series of sacrifices with 15 to 11. Black has to jump from 8 to 15 (7 to 16 would give White an immediate double jump from 20 to 11 to 4 and a king). Then White sacrifices again from 30 to 25 and Black leaps into the king row from 21 to 30. Still another White sacrifice from 20 to 16 forces the Black checker on 12 to jump to 19 and White jumps right back from 23 to 16. Now Black's new king leaps from 30 to 23, giving White's man on 27 a winning triple vault to 18 to 9 to 2, where he receives a crown. From there, White should have no trouble wiping out the poorly positioned Black army.

6. Black starts with 14 to 17 and White can jump from 2 to 9 or 21 to 14. After White takes whichever jump he wants, Black moves from 19 to 23 and White must execute the other aforementioned jump. Next Black sacrifices with 23 to 27, so White leaps from 32 to 23 to set Black up for a victorious position after he carries out his triple bound from 26 to 19 to 10 to 17. The White checker on 28 is trapped and the White king on square 9 can only move to 5. Black's king will force White to give up the checker on 13 in a couple of moves and quickly flush the White king out of the double corner for the win (unless White resigns to save time). Great Black tactics!

7. Black begins with 3 to 8 and White's king jumps from 4 to 11. Then Black moves the White king on

11 further up the board by going from 10 to 15 so the White king leaps to 18. That's it! Black gets a king with 27 to 32 and also forces White's king on 20 to jump to 27. This positions Black's new monarch for a quadruple capturing spree from 32 to 23 to 14 to 21 to 30. From there, Black will be able to stalk and capture the White checkers as they make their tortured way down the board. An amazing recovery for Black!

8. Black moves from 20 to 24 and White jumps from 28 to 19 to prevent Black from getting a king. Next Black sacrifices from 3 to 8 and White's monarch on 4 leaps to 11. Now, when Black slides in from 25 to 30 for his crown, White has to jump from 10 to 1. That provides Black with a triple capturing bound from 30 to 23 to 16 to 7. White's lost! If he goes from 1 to 6, Black will move into the breech to capture yet another White piece. Any move by the White checker on 15 is suicidal.

9. White wins with a wicked series of sacrifices that eventually devastates the Black ranks as follows: White goes 9 to 6 and Black jumps 1 to 10. White sacrifices again with 30 to 26 and Black leaps into the king row from 21 to 30. Then White gives up the checker on 26 to the newly crowned monarch by moving from 24 to 20. After the Black king hops to

23, White gets a double vault from 20 to 11 to 4 and a king of his own. Then Black has to take the 18-to-25 capture, which sets White up for a 27-to-18-to-11-to-2 triple jump and another king, so Black doesn't stand a chance.

10. Black moves from 21 to 25, so White jumps from 30 to 21. Next Black goes from 11 to 16 and White must leap from 17 to 10, which opens up two double-jumping opportunities for Black. He selects 6 to 15 to 24 and White gets a reciprocal jump from 28 to 19. That positions Black for another double capture from 16 to 23 to 30 and a king! From there it's a simple mopping-up exercise for the win. Note: If White had taken the 17 to 10 jump first, Black would have executed the 6-to-24 double jump and after White jumped back from 28 to 19, Black would have moved from 11 to 16 to get the game-winning double jump into the king row as soon as White took the forced capture from 30 to 21.

11. White startles Black by moving from 13 to 9, giving Black a double jump from 6 to 13 to 22. White leaps back from 26 to 17 and Black has to capture with 19 to 26 or 18 to 27. Either will provide White with a triple jump from 31 to 6. From there he'll get a king on his next move and chase down the disadvantaged

Black checkers for a fine win. Note: If Black chose 18 to 27 for his first jump, White would leap from 9 to 2 for a king and an even stronger position.

12. Black starts with 16 to 19 and White jumps from 23 to 16. Then Black moves from 11 to 15, so White hops from 18 to 11. Next Black leaves his back row with 2 to 6 and White leaps right in from 11 to 2 and receives a crown. But now, when Black slides from 28 to 32 for his own king, White's comeuppance is at hand. After White's new monarch jumps from 2 to 9, Black's fledgling sovereign captures five White pieces in a quintuple jump from 32 to 23 to 30 to 21 to 14 and finally to 5. From the resulting position, Black's royal highness and his two-man army defeat the hapless White remnants in just a few more moves.

13. White moves from 19 to 16 and Black has to double-jump from 12 to 26 or from 28 to 26. After Black makes whichever one of these he chooses, White moves his king from 2 to 6. Now Black must jump from 12 to 19 or from 28 to 19, depending on which double jump he took on his previous turn. As soon as he takes whichever one is available, White whips around the board with a sextuple leap in either direction and ends up back on square 6 to capture the last Black checker on its next move.

14. White is taken aback when Black goes from 3 to 8 to give his king on 4 a leap to 11. Another Black sacrifice from 10 to 15 forces the same king to jump to 18. Then, when Black slides into the king row from 27 to 32, White gets another capture from 20 to 27. That puts Black's new monarch into a quadruple bound from 32 to 23 to 14 to 21 to 30 and he's trapped both of White's two remaining pieces for a dramatic victory.

15. Black starts with 11 to 16, so White takes the 13-to-6 jump. Then Black goes from 15 to 18 and White leaps from 22 to 15. Black jumps back from 10 to 19 and White reciprocates with 24 to 15. That provides Black with a double jump from 1 to 10 to 19 and a solid winning position. Wherever White goes gives Black another jump and he'll soon have a king to beat down the already depleted White team for the win.

16. Black begins with 14 to 17 and White must jump from 21 to 14. Then Black moves his king from 32 to 28 so White has to leap from 30 to 21. Next Black sacrifices from 7 to 11. Now either the White king hops from 8 to 15 or the White checker on 16 jumps to 7. It doesn't matter which capturing play White selects because right afterward Black will sacrifice again from 24 to 27 and go on a sextuple vaulting/capturing sprint from 28 to 12 right after

White hops from 31 to 24. A resounding triumph for Black!

17. Black sets up the win with a series of sacrifices starting with 11 to 15 and White must jump from 18 to 11. That gives Black's king a 16-to-7 capture and leaves White with only one safe move from 5 to 1 for a second king. Black goes from 6 to 9 and White must jump from 14 to 5. Then Black moves his king from 7 to 10 and White is stymied. Every move he makes will lead to a capture and, in the case of 1 to 6, it also leads to a block after Black's king jumps from 10 to 1.

18. Black's first move is from 4 to 8 and White's king jumps from 3 to 12. Then Black goes from 11 to 16 and White makes another capture with 20 to 11. Now Black moves his king on 31 to 26. White's monarch on 1 has to jump to 10. After that, Black's sovereign on 19 slides to 16, where he's captured by White's king on 12 leaping to 19. That sets up Black's king on 23 for a game-busting quintuple vault to 16 to 7 to 14 to 21 to 30 and it's all over! Note: If White had taken the 1-to-10 jump first, Black would have moved his king on 31 to 26 and after White had jumped from 3 to 12, Black would have sacrificed from 11 to 16 and ended up with the same quintuple game-winner.

19. White's king moves from 6 to 10 and Black has to go from 14 to 17 to avoid being jumped. Next White plays 10 to 15 so Black jumps 17 to 26. After that, White gives up his checker on 27 by moving it to 24 and Black jumps from 20 to 27. Then White sacrifices again from 19 to 16 and Black leaps from 12 to 19. That positions White's king for a triple hop, skip, and jump from 15 to 24 to 31 to 22, where he pins Black's king on 29 and the Black checker on 13. From this position, White will quickly stifle the Black checker on 8 as he tries to make his way up the board. Nice going, White!

20. Black's first move is 1 to 6, and White's king on 2 jumps to 9. Then Black goes from 20 to 24 so White leaps from 28 to 19. Next Black sacrifices from 12 to 16 and White has to capture from 19 to 12. Still another Black sacrifice from 11 to 8 with his king forces White to leap from 12 to 3, where he obtains a fourth king. But when Black slides in from 27 to 31 for his own monarch, White's newest sovereign must jump from 3 to 10. That sets Black up for a sextuple victory vault from 31 to 22 to 13 to 6 to 15 to 22 and on to 29. From there he tracks down the lone White checker on square 30 in five relentless moves. Almost unbelievable.

21. Black moves 19 to 24 and White's king on 5 jumps to 14. Then Black goes from 15 to 18 and the same White king leaps to 23. Next Black moves from 16 to 19 and the White king gets another capture with 23 to 16. Now Black slides from 24 to 27 and White jumps from 32 to 23. The trap is set and sprung when Black moves his king from 22 to 17. White must jump from 29 to 22 to provide Black with a sensational sextuple bounding exercise from 17 to 26 to 19 to 12 to 3 to 10 to 1. From the resulting position it's a simple cleanup effort for the outright win. Note: If White had jumped from 31 to 24, instead of 32 to 23, Black would have jumped back from 20 to 27 and then White would have to make the 32-to-23 capture leading to the same end result.

22. Black forces the White checker on 18 all around the board on a merciless mission that positions Black for a sensational quintuple jump for a beautiful win. He starts with 11 to 15 and White jumps from 18 to 11. Then Black goes from 2 to 7 and White hops in from 11 to 2 for a king. Next Black sacrifices again from 3 to 7, so the new White king leaps back out from 2 to 11. Black follows with yet another sacrifice from 12 to 16 that forces the same White king to jump from 11 to 20. Now comes the coup de grâce when Black slides into the king row from 27 to 32 and White's king on 20 has to hop to 27. This gives

Black's new monarch a glorious victory vault from 32 to 23 to 30 to 21 to 14 to 5. Magnifique!

23. Black starts with 21 to 25 and White jumps 30 to 21. Then Black goes 14 to 17 and White's king jumps again from 21 to 14. Now Black sacrifices once more with 5 to 9 and the same White king leaps to 5. A fourth consecutive Black sacrifice from 7 to 10 forces White to hop from 16 to 7 and the stage is set. Black goes 13 to 9 and White's king on 5 vaults to 14. This puts Black in position for a triple bound from 10 to 17 to 26 to 19. White's king on 24 jumps to 15, giving Black's monarch on 3 a final double jump to 10 and on to 19, where he pins down White's two remaining checkers for a mind-boggling triumph!

24. White moves 21 to 17 and the Black king on 14 jumps to 21. That gives White's king on 5 a double jump to 7, where he in turn is jumped by Black's checker on 2, who hops to 11. That gives White's king on 8 a double jump to 15 to 24, where he's captured by the Black checker on 20, who leaps to 27. White's monarch on 32 double-jumps to 23 to 30 and when Black's king on 21 moves to 17 (the only move he has), that last White sovereign gets another double leap from 30 to 21 to 14. From there he traps Black's lone king in two more obvious moves. What a chain reaction!

25. White sacrifices the checker on 18 by moving it to 15 and Black jumps from 11 to 18. Then White sacrifices again with 14 to 10 and Black jumps from 6 to 15. White leaps back from 23 to 14, so Black has to capture from 16 to 23, which gives White a triple victory vault from 27 to 18 to 11 to 4 and, after conducting a routine cleanup operation, he has a well-deserved triumph.

26. Black sacrifices his king on 23 by moving it to 18, and White's king on 14 has to jump to 23. Then Black gives up his man on 5 by moving him to 9 so White's king on 13 must jump to 6. That provides Black's monarch on square 1 with a game-winning quadruple vault to 10 to 19 to 26 and, finally, to 17. Well played!

27. Black startles White by moving from 14 to 17 and White must jump from 21 to 14 to 7 or from 5 to 14 to 7 with his king. It doesn't matter which double leap White takes because right afterward Black moves his king on 31 to 27. Then White has to jump whichever Black checker he left on the board (21 to 14 or 5 to 14). That sets Black up for a fantastic, sextuple, board-cleaning victory vault from 27 to 20 to 11 to 2 to 9 to 18 and back to 27 (or in the opposite direction from 27 to 18 to 9 to 2 to 11 to 20 and back to 27). A fabulous win for a very resourceful player who wouldn't give up!

28. Black begins with a 14-to-18 sacrifice and White has to jump from 22 to 15. Then Black sacrifices a second time with 5 to 9 and White sees the handwriting on the wall, but it's too late. He must capture from 13 to 6 and set Black off on a board-clearing triple-jump spree from 1 to 10 to 19 to 28.

29. White simply moves from 26 to 23 and Black has to jump from 18 to 27, but when White makes his next move from 29 to 25, Black has no move to make so he loses the game to a very opportunistic opponent.

30. Black slides from 1 to 6 and White's only safe move is from 5 to 1. It doesn't prove to be safe at all after Black sacrifices with 6 to 9 and the White checker on 14 leaps to 5, because Black's king then moves from 7 to 10 and ends the game. White can only move his king to 6, where it will be captured by Black's monarch's leaping to 1 and blocking the remaining White checker on 5 from going anywhere. Neat.

31. White sacrifices 11 to 7, so Black has to jump from 3 to 10. Then White moves from 2 to 7 and wherever Black goes he'll set up a game-winning double jump for White. Note: White could also start with 11 to 8 and after Black jumps from 3 to 12, White could sacrifice his king on 6 by moving it to 10 and get a double jump to square 18 no matter which way Black captured. From there he'd track down the Black checker in two moves for the win, proving there's more than one way to skin a cat.

32. Black shoots his stun gun at White by sacrificing on his first move with 7 to 11, and White has to jump 16 to 7. But then when Black moves his king from 6 to 2, White only has one move he can make, which is 3 to 8 with his king, and that gives Black a double-leaping victory when he vaults from 2 to 11 to 4.

33. Black startles White with 11 to 8, sacrificing his king! White jumps from 12 to 3, where he gets a crown for a king that ends his turn. Then Black slides from 27 to 31 for a king, and White's recently crowned sovereign must jump from 3 to 10. That gives Black's royal highness a board-clearing triple bound over all three White kings from 31 to 22 to 15 to 6. Very nice work!

1. Red in the face.

2. $325 = 1^2 + 18^2 = 6^2 + 17^2 = 10^2 + 15^2$.

3. I would not want a tiger to chase me or a zebra to chase me. Given the choice, I'd rather a tiger chased a zebra, not me.

4. Eleven students passed Exam One only, three passed Exam Two only, and eight passed Exam Three only. Thus ten students passed more than one exam.

5. Square meal.

6. $\sqrt{.2^{-2}}$, which shows that two twos can make five!

7. For White to win, he has to force one of Black's knights to move. Then, provided White's king is safe from unwanted checks and White has not moved his own knights, White wins with Ne4 mate or Nd5 mate. The actual winning move will depend upon which knight Black eventually moves.

Black can delay moving a knight for 59 moves! His tactic is to shunt the rook at a4 to and fro to a3 whenever he can. Accordingly, and taking the route that avoids unwanted checks, White uses his king to inhibit the shunting rook by timing the arrival of his king at b5 to follow Black's move Ra3.

On the first four occasions White does this, Black keeps his rook out of danger by moving a pawn on the e file. On the fifth occasion, to avoid moving a knight and to save his rook, Black must block his rook in with a5-a4. On his next move Black is compelled to move a knight and expose himself to an instant checkmate. Note that if Black moves his pawns before he has to, then the mate is simply speeded up. With Black's best defense as shown below, White will mate in sixty.

White's first move can be either Ke8 or Kd6. White's king then proceeds d7, c8, b7, b6, b5. By moving to d7 via e8 or d6, the White king arrives at b5 after an even number of moves. Thus, for move six, Black's shunting rook will be at a3 and Black must move a pawn, lose his rook, or be mated. To defer mate as long as possible, Black must play e4-e3.

After Black's move, e4-e3, White moves his king away from b5 and Black can continue with the shunting of his rook. White must now move his king back to b5 in an odd number of moves in order to catch the shunting rook at a3. The shortest route for White to achieve this that avoids unwanted checks is b6, b7, c8, d7, e8, f8, f7, e8, d7, c8, b7, b6, b5, and this he repeats four times. On moves 19, 32, and 45 Black takes a break from shunting his rook and moves a pawn on the e file. On move 58, however, Black can do no better than to block his rook in with a5-a4. White then plays a waiting move, Kb6. If Black moves the knight at b4, then White mates with Nd5, and if Black moves the knight at d2, then White mates with Ne4. This gives White mate in sixty.

8. No U-Turn.

9. 2,100,010,006.

10. e^{π} is greater than π^e. To two decimal places, $e^{\pi} = 23.14$ and $\pi^e = 22.46$.

11. AAKAAKKK.

12. The players scored 5, 7, 11, 13, 17, 19, 29, 31, 37, 41, and 43 goals. Their average was 23 goals.

13. By changing his mind, B reduced his chance of winning the game.

The only way in which EEE can appear before OEE is if the first three throws of the die are EEE. Otherwise the sequence EEE must be preceded by an O. The probability of the first three throws being E is $(\frac{1}{2})^3$, so if B chooses OEE when A has chosen EEE, then B wins with probability $\frac{7}{8}$. If B chooses OOO in response to A's choice of EEE, then B's chance of winning is $\frac{1}{2}$.

14. 11, 47, and 71.

15. Round of drinks on the house.

16. Smith served first. One possible proof is as follows:

Whoever served first would have served on 20 of the points played and the other player would have served on 17 of them. Suppose the first player won x of the points on which he served and y of the points served by his opponent. The total number of points lost by the player who served them is then $20 - x + y$. This must equal 13, since we are told that 24 of the 37 points were won by the player serving. Thus $x = 7 + y$, and the first server won $(7 + y) + y = 7 + 2y$ points in total. This is an odd number, and only Smith won an odd number of points. Thus Smith served first.

17. White's key move of 1 Ka5!! seems self-destructive and a sure provocation for Black to play 1 ... e1(Q)+. White's reply, 2 Kb6!, seems even more provocative as it offers Black no fewer than seven different moves with which to check White's king. Each one, however, can be defended by moving the knight at c6 for a discovered checkmate. If Black moves 1 ... Rg7, then 2 Ne7+ Ka7 3 Nc8 mate. If 1 ... Rg5, then

2 Kb6 (threatening 3 Ne7 mate) Rxd5 3 Nc7 mate. If
1 … Kb7, then 2 Ne7+ Ka7 3 Nc8 mate.

18. The series is generated by counting the number of
characters in the corresponding Roman numeral, as
shown for the first ten numbers below:

I	II	III	IV	V	VI	VII	VIII	IX	X
1	2	3	2	1	2	3	4	2	1

The first term to equal 10 is the 288th in the series:
CCLXXXVIII. Thus the answer to the question is
Brutus.

19. Forever and ever.

20. Either 1, 2, 6, 7, 9, 14, 15, 18, 20 or 1, 3, 6, 7, 12,
14, 15, 19, 20.

21. The traveler on the fast train sees all the trains
going the other way around that left up to three hours
ago or that will leave in the next two hours. The traveler on the slow train sees all the trains going the other
way around that left up to two hours ago or that will
leave in the next three hours. In five hours, including
the beginning and end, 21 trains depart in each direction. Including the train they are traveling on, each
traveler therefore sees 22 trains on his journey.

22. Mixed bag.

23. The minimum number of moves made by White's men to reach the position shown in the question is: queen's pawn 5 (d4, c5, b6, a7, a8), new queen 2 (a7, e3), queen's knight 2 (c3, a4), king's knight 2 (f3, h2), king's rook 2 (h3, g3), king's rook's pawn 2 (h3, g4), king's bishop's pawn 1 (f3), and king 1 (f2). These total seventeen and therefore account for all of White's moves. Noting that Black's missing pieces were captured on c5, b6, a7, and g4, the position after White's ninth move would have been as follows:

The game from White's ninth move was:

9	...	Ra7	14	Nh2	a5
10	bxa7	h4	15	f3	a4
11	a8(Q)	h3	16	Kf2	a3
12	Qa7	h2	17	Na4	
13	Qe3	h1(B)			

24. The letter m.

25. There are 120 socks in the drawer: 85 red ones and 35 blue ones.

26. At the point of no return.

27. White marbles can only be removed from the box in pairs. There is an odd number of white marbles to start with, so the last marble in the box will be white.

28. 72 hens, 21 sheep, 7 cows.

29. F for February. The letters are the initials of the first eight months of the year.

30. Pin-up.

31. The solutions are the numbers 1,872,549,630 and 7,812,549,630, and are derived as follows: The 5 and 0 can be placed immediately. The sixth digit must be 4. The seventh digit is odd (since every second digit must be even), so it must be 9. The eighth digit must be 6. The ninth digit must be 3. The third digit is 1 or 7, so the fourth digit must be 2. The first three digits are therefore 187 or 781.

32. Supplements to use are: 8, 12, 14, 17, 18, 19, 20, 21, 22, 23, 25, 26, 27, 29, 30, 31, 33, 35, 37, 39, 41, 43, 45, 47, and 49. They total 711.

33. Queueing.

34. The value of 1,997 nickels is $99.85, 25 cents more than 1,992 nickels (worth $99.60).

35. One step forward, two steps back.

36. 8128.

37. Regrouping the series as 1, 2, 4, 8, 16, 32, 64, 128, and 256, the next two terms in this series are 512 and 1024. The answer to the question is 5121.

38. Bermuda Triangle.

39. The maximum number of blocks in the set is 55.

If only three of the five available colors are used, then opposite faces of a block must have the same color. Thus by symmetry there is only one way in which a block can be painted with any three given colors, and there are 10 different ways in which three colors can be chosen.

If four colors are used, then two pairs of opposite faces must each have the same color. By symmetry it doesn't matter which way around the other two faces are painted. The colors for the two pairs of matching faces can be chosen in ten different ways, and the other two colors can then be chosen in three ways, giving an overall total of 30 combinations.

Finally, if five colors are used then just one pair of opposite faces will have the same color. The remaining four colors can be arranged in three different ways, so using five colors gives a total of $5 \times 3 = 15$ combinations.

The maximum number of blocks in the set is therefore $10 + 30 + 15 = 55$.

40. There are 26 former committee members (9 of whom are women), 27 committee members, and 39 members who have never been on the committee. This gives a total of 92 members.

41. The series consists of the numbers of letters in the words one, two, three, etc.

42. The integers are −3, −1, and 1.

43. Old is 30 and Young is 18.

44. Anyone for tennis?

Two by Two (page 278)

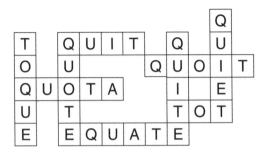

Two by Two (page 279)

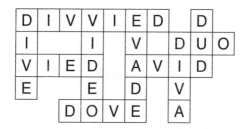

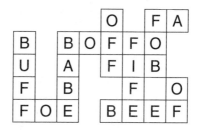

Mixagrams (pages 280–281)

SHUSH + DEBT   FOIST + LOBE
SCROD + EDIT   OUTER + CLIP
AMEND + GORE   URGES + COTS
USAGE + ENDS   RECUR + COST
SONG BIRD   FOUR BITS

Two by Two (page 282)

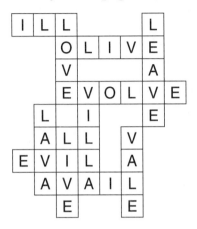

Two by Two (page 283)

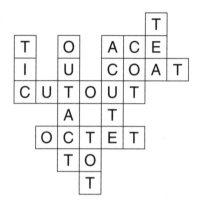

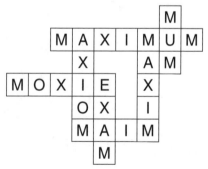

Latticework (pages 284–285)

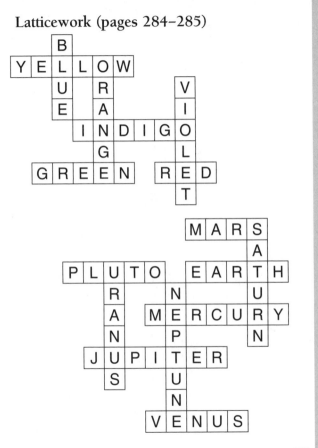

Two by Two (page 286)

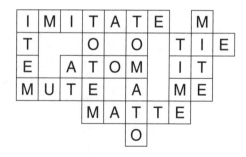

Two by Two (page 287)

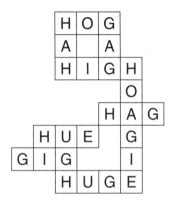

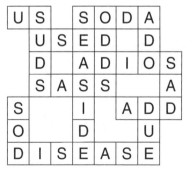

Mixagrams (pages 288–289)

WHORL + PACE	SWIFT + ITEM
BALSA + ALES	ARROW + DINE
BLEAT + SAGE	SHRUG + UPON
TENSE + SOAP	CHILI + ASPS
LATE PASS	FOUL TIPS

Two by Two (page 290)

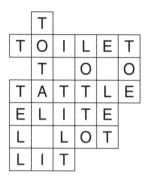

Two by Two (page 291)

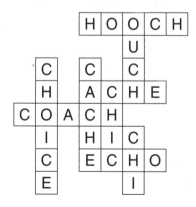

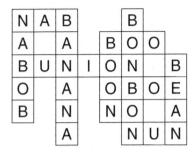

Mixagrams (pages 292–293)

ETHIC + RICE	LOWER + SHOD
CRANE + ONTO	ALIGN + HOOD
TORSO + CHOW	FENCE + OGRE
RADAR + KING	ADEPT + PIER
HARD ROCK	WINE SHOP

Fill-in Station (pages 294–295)

W	E	B
H	O	E
O	N	E

S	A	C
H	U	E
E	K	E

Two by Two (page 296)

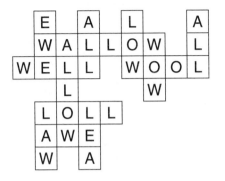

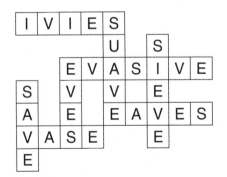

Two by Two (page 297)

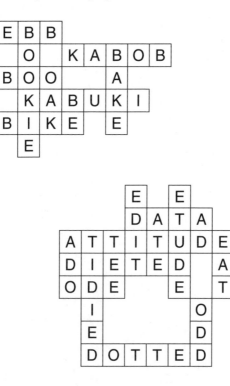

Clueless Crosswords (page 298–299)

Mixagrams (pages 300–301)

TRACK + ANEW   GAUZE + SPOT
COUPE + HERO   BERET + OVAL
LAPSE + POOR   BRUSH + ABET
ADDLE + PEAK   PUTTY + POOL
ROAD WORK   ZEST SOAP

Two by Two (page 302)

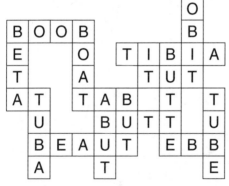

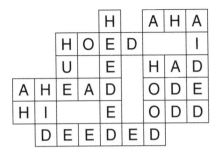

Two by Two (page 303)

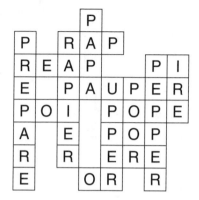

Latticework
(pages 304–305)

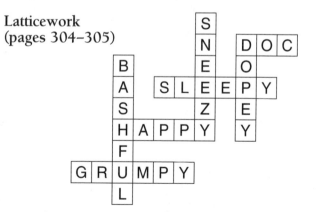

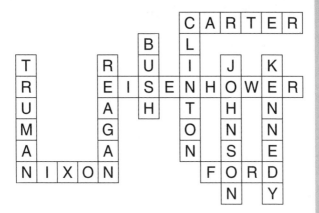

Mixagrams (pages 306–307)

CLOUD + THEM   SEDAN + LADY

KAPPA + MITE   LILAC + SOUP

ALTAR + ARIA   ALIAS + SYNC

SPOOK + ABUT   MOGUL + BIKE

DARK MEAT   SLAM DUNK

Fill-in Station (pages 308–309)

S	O	P
E	A	R
W	R	Y

A	P	E
I	L	K
L	Y	E

Two by Two (page 310)

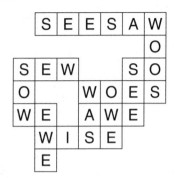

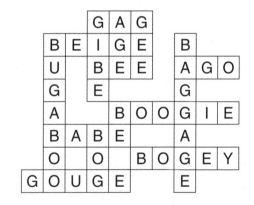

Two by Two (page 311)

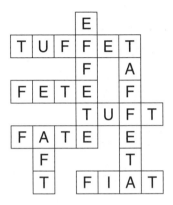

Clueless Crosswords (pages 312–313)

S K I M P E D
T · G · L · I
A N N U A L S
M · E · Q · P
P R O F U S E
E · U · E · L
D E S I S T S

B E Q U E S T
R · U · M · U
A M A T E U R
I · R · R · K
N I T R A T E
E · E · L · Y
D I R N D L S

1. Only once, because the second time you will be subtracting from 24 instead of 30.

2. The number 8. (It is made up of two zeroes, one on top of the other.)

3. By using Roman numerals. The upper half of XII is VII.

4. 1 and 9.

5. Any number and 1.

6. 2 and 2.

7. It is easy to eliminate possibilities. For example, it has to be an even number; none of the digits can be zero (or else the product would be zero); and the product of the digits must be less than or equal to 48 (otherwise two times the product would have three digits). If you think of the remaining possibilities, you will find the answer, $36 = 2 \times 3 \times 6$.

8. 1, 2, and 3, because $1 \times 2 \times 3 = 1 + 2 + 3 = 6$.

9. $25 = 5^2$ and $36 = 6^2$.

10. $9^{9^9} = 9^{387420489}$, which is a number with more than 369 million digits.

11. The father is 41 and the son is 14.

12. 10 cents.

13. $1.10 for the outlet and $0.10 for the lightbulb.

14. $3 \times 75 = 225$ qualities distributed among 100 persons, so at least 25% of them have all three.

15. The number of passing grades is a whole number less than 32, and 5% of it is also a whole number. It can only be 20. If 20 is the number of passing grades, the number of students from New York that took the test is one.

16. If half of the 83% tipped the usher 10 cents and the other half didn't, it is the same as if all 83% had tipped him 5 cents, which is the same amount as what the remaining 17% tipped. The usher received 4,800 cents, or more simply, 48 dollars.

17. Turn the page upside-down. It will read $108 = 6 \times 18$.

18. He will need twenty "9's," one for the numbers 9, 19, 29, 39, 49, 59, 69, 79, 89, 90, 91, 92, 93, 94, 95, 96, 97, and 98, and two for 99.

19. At each stop, passengers can buy a ticket for any of the 24 remaining stops. Therefore, the number of tickets will be $25 \times 24 = 600$.

20. Let's imagine that the inhabitants are as different as possible (one will be bald, another will have only one hair, another two, another three, and so on, until we get to someone having 100,000 hairs). Inhabitant number 100,002 will have the same number of hairs as someone among the first 100,001 inhabitants. The total population is more than 200,000 people, which means that there will be more than 100,000 inhabitants with the same number of hairs as other people in town.

21. Three: one red, one blue, and one brown.

22. There are 6 chestnut trees per side, making a total of 12.

23. Two birds and one olive tree.

24. There is only one winner, so the remaining 110 players were defeated in 110 matches. Therefore, they used 110 balls.

25. Twelve muffins. When John ate half the remaining muffins plus three more to leave none, he must have eaten six muffins. So Peter ate half the muffins and left six, meaning that there were twelve to start.

26. The shepherd that is talking had 5 sheep and the other one had 7.

27. Three cages and four canaries.

28. Each sardine costs 1 dollar. Therefore, 7½ sardines would cost 7½ dollars.

29. Since ½ brick weighs 3 pounds, 1½ bricks weigh 9 pounds.

30. Since 18 sardines is the same as 1½ dozen, they cost 9½ dollars.

31. Since 1 man eats 1 pie in 1½ minutes, 1 man eats 20 pies in 30 minutes, which means 3 men eat 60 pies in 30 minutes.

32. 11 times (one fewer than the number of times he went in).

33. Three ducks.

34. The person who won three games must have also lost six games, since his opponent won $3. In total, they played 9 games.

35. We measure the inside diameter and the height of the liquid, obtaining the volume of the liquid. Then, we turn the bottle upside down and measure the volume of the empty part. If we add both, we obtain the total capacity of the bottle and can calculate the percentage of the liquid. An easier way is to measure only both heights, because both have the same size base.

36. $0.0125.

37. By leaving a task half done (for example, peeling potatoes) so that the next soldier can finish it, they can do all the tasks in 1 hour and 30 minutes.

38. 29 days. One spider would have covered half of the space on the 29th day, and on the 30th day would repeat what had been done, covering the space completely. Two spiders would each have covered half of the space in 29 days, therefore covering the entire area.

39. At 8 P.M. Each hour the volume triples, so it is one-third full one hour before it is full.

40. If the length of the rope + 2 yards = 3 times the length of the rope, then the rope is 1 yard long.

41. If the length is 6 yards + half the length, then half the length is 6 yards. Therefore, it is 12 yards long.

42. No mud at all, because a hole can only contain air.

43. There are only three people, a daughter, her mother, and her grandmother. The mother received 25 books from the grandmother and then gave 8 to her daughter.

44. Dolores is taller than Emily, who is taller than Ann.

45. Joan is 6 years older than Rose.

46. Emily speaks in a softer voice than Dolores (Emily < Ann < Dolores).

47. Peter is sitting between Philip (on his right) and James (on his left).

48. A pound of $10 gold coins has twice the amount of gold than half a pound of $20 coins. Therefore, it is worth more.

49. The store lost $40 given as change plus the value of the umbrella, $10. The transaction was only between the sales person and the customer. The bank teller did not take part in the transaction.

50. The pitcher with water contains exactly the same amount of wine as water in the pitcher of wine. Both pitchers have the same volume of liquid before and after mixing water and wine, so mixing them makes no difference.

51. He made each candidate ride another candidate's horse. Each one would, of course, try to come in first, because in that way the owner of the horse that a particular candidate was riding would lose the race.

52. The weight of the fishbowl increases by the same amount as the weight of the liquid displaced by the fish.

53. If it is a traditional scale with two dishes, you can place the apples in one dish and dirt in the other until they balance. Then, replace the apples with weights and you will know the weight of the apples. If it is a spring scale, you weigh the apples first, then write down the mark on the scale and replace the apples with weights until you reach the previous mark. The weights will show the real weight of the apples.

54. The reaction of the air that the little bird is pushing down in order to fly will partially affect both the dish of the scale and the floor of the room. The scale will show one pound minus some portion of the 5 ounces that the bird weighs.

If the cage were sealed, the air would affect only the dish of the scale and the scale would continue to read one pound.

55. One weighing. Take one ball from the first sack, two from the second, three from the third, and so on until you reach the last sack, from which you take ten balls. Since $1 + 2 + 3 + ... + 9 + 10 = 55$, if all of the balls weighed 10 ounces each, the total weight would be 550 ounces. In this case, the weight will be 550 – N, where N is the number of the sack containing nine-ounce balls.

56. We identify each sack by the number of balls taken from it. We must find a way to obtain different results from all possible sums of the digits that identify the sacks. The easiest way would be powers of 2: 1, 2, 4, 8, 16, ... (2^0, 2^1, 2^2, 2^3, 2^4, ...). Therefore, we will take one ball from one sack, two from another, four from another, etc.

The resulting weight will be 1023 – N, where N can only be obtained by adding certain sack numbers. If N is 27 ounces, the sacks containing 9-ounce balls will be those from which we took 1, 2, 8, and 16 balls, because, using just the powers of 2, 27 can only be obtained by adding $1 + 2 + 8 + 16$.

Let's call "1" the sack from which we took 1 ball, "2" the one from which we took 2 balls, "3" the one from which we took 4 balls, etc. The number 27, in binary, is 11011. The position of the 1's in this binary sequence reveals the solution. The 1's are in first, second, fourth, and fifth position, which means that the sacks containing the 9-ounce balls are 1, 2, 4, and 5.

57. The best solution is to open four links from one of the pieces and use them to join the remaining five parts in one chain. The total cost will be $4 \times 60 = 240$ cents, or \$2.40.

58. By cutting the third link, we obtain three pieces of one, two, and four links each. The first day, she pays with the one-link part. The second day, she pays with the two-link part and gets the one-link piece back as change. The third day, she pays with the loose link. The fourth day, she pays with the four-link part and receives back the three links, and so on.

59. The minimum number of parts that could have been left is 3 (the link that is cut and the two disconnected parts of the chain). The maximum number will be 6, as shown in the figure below.

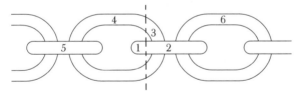

60. Two glasses. Pick up the second glass, pour its contents into the ninth glass, and put it back. Then pick up the fourth glass, pour its contents into the seventh glass, and put it back. Note that the seventh and ninth glasses are not moved.

61. 100% probability, because if four marbles are in their corresponding cups, the fifth one must be in its corresponding cup, too.

62. Three. The first two can be of different colors, white and black, but the third sock will be one of these two colors, and thus complete one pair.

63. Four. There are three different colors, so the first three socks may not match, but the fourth one will match one of the previous three socks.

64. 13. The first 12 gloves can be six white left gloves and six black left gloves. Therefore, the 13th glove will make a pair with one of the previous 12 gloves. No matter what the first 12 gloves are, if no two have made a pair yet, the 13th will.

65. 6. The worst case is to take two white, two black, and the red marble. The sixth marble has to be either white or black.

66. Put five marbles in one cup, four in another, and one in another. Put the cup with one marble inside the one containing four. There are other solutions, all based on the same trick. Another solution, for example, involves putting three marbles in one cup, three marbles in the second cup, and four marbles in the third cup, and then putting the second cup inside the third one. This leaves three marbles in the first cup, three marbles in the second cup, and seven marbles in the third cup.

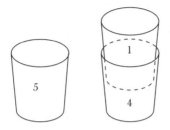

67. Put one marble in one box, three in another, and five in a third one. Then place the three boxes inside the fourth box.

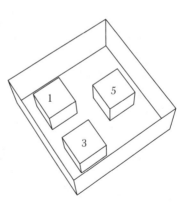

68. Take one marble from the box marked BW. If it is white, the other marble must also be white. This means that the box marked BB must have black and white marbles and the box marked WW must have only black marbles. You can apply the same principle if the first marble you take is black.

69. After being inverted twice, the hourglass continued working in its initial position. Therefore, the extra hour that it measured was a consequence of these two inversions, half an hour each time. If it was inverted for the second time at 11:30, the first time had to be a half-hour earlier, at 11:00.

70. The clock that doesn't work will show the precise time twice a day, but the fast one will take $2 \times 60 \times 12 = 1440$ days to show the precise time. Therefore, the broken clock shows the correct time more often.

71. Time to have the clock fixed.

72. Ten times (you can verify it yourself).

73. Four seconds (it takes two seconds between 2 consecutive strikes).

74. Four hours, the time between 8 and 12.

75. There is 1 second between 2 strikes. Therefore, it will take 11 seconds for the clock to strike 12 times.

76. He lived 59 years, because there is no "0" year.

77. He would have drunk the same number of cups of coffee. The difference is that the conversation would have taken place on March 14.

78. Friday.

79. Three days and two nights. She left yesterday and will return tomorrow.

80. The man's birthday is December 31 and he was talking on January 1. He's 36 now, the day before yesterday he was 35, this calendar year he will turn 37, and next calendar year he will turn 38.

81. It happened to Gioacchino Rossini, who was born on February 29, 1792, and who died on November 13, 1868. Remember that 1800 was not a leap year. All years that are divisible by four are leap years, except those that end in "00." They are only leap years if they are divisible by 400.

82. INVENT.

83. Neither. The yolk of an egg is yellow.

84. It is not "I am going in" or "I am not going in." The opposite is "I am leaving."

85. The word "incorrectly."

86. Lounger.

87. It's a matter of language. Consider "four twenty" as $4.20. Then it is true.

88. Yes. "Paris" starts with a "p," and "ends" starts with an "e."

89. The phone operator was trying to get the spelling of the man's last name. Therefore it makes no sense to ask, "I as in what?" The operator had already understood it was an "I."

90. The letter "i."

91. Let's suppose it is false. By saying "This statement is false," it becomes true and vice versa. Therefore, to be false it has to be true and vice versa. It is a paradox.

92. The letter "u."

93. He will not change his mind.

94. His statement must be "I will be hanged." If they want to hang him, the sentence is true, and therefore, they will not be able to hang him. For the same reason, he cannot be drowned because his statement would be false and they could not drown him if his statement is false. (Based on *Don Quixote*, by Cervantes.)

95. Yes, as long as the other half are male, too. She has five sons.

96. Nine children.

97. Three more brothers than sisters. Ann's brother has one more brother than sister. Ann is one of the sisters, so Ann will have one fewer sister than her brother has and one more brother than her brother has.

98. Seven. The only possible solution is that the person talking is a woman and there are four women and three men.

99. The doctor is a woman.

100. John is Raymond's son.

101. Your mother.

102. The son's mother.

103. The second man is Charles's grandson.

104. No, because it would be his mother.

105. The man is Ann's uncle.

106. If the man left a widow, then he is dead. Therefore, he cannot get married.

107. She was looking at a photo of her nephew.

108. He was looking at a photo of his father.

109. Two widowers have one daughter each and decide to marry each other's daughters. This conversation takes place once they are married and with children. Their wives are the ones talking.

1. Twins

I spoke to Peter. If a person always lies or, alternately, always tells the truth, he cannot admit that he is lying (if this person were a liar, he would be telling the truth, and if this person were honest, he would be lying). Therefore, Paul could not have answered my question. Peter could answer about Paul without contradicting himself. What we don't know is who the liar is.

2. Twin Statistics

More than 3% of the population are twins. Out of 100 births, 97 are single and 3 are twins. That's 103 babies in total, 6 of which are twins, which represents 5.8% of the population.

3. The Professor and His Friend

Professor Zizoloziz wins. Every player takes an odd number of matches per play. After the first player goes, there will always be an odd number of matches left. After the second player goes, there will always be an even number of matches left. Therefore, the second player is the winner.

4. Irregular Circuit

300 yards from point A. The first passing point can be considered as a new starting point. Therefore, the new passing point will be 150 yards away.

5. Economical Progression

1, 6, 11, 16, 21, 26. Other solutions are also possible.

6. Skin and Shoes

It is enough to look at only one shoe. If, for example, the white man's right shoe is red, the left one has to be black. This means that the black man will have one left red shoe and one right white shoe, and so on.

7. Up and Down

22 steps. While Zizoloziz goes up the entire staircase, I descend the staircase except for 11 steps (7 at the top + 4 at the bottom). Since he goes twice as fast as me, the entire staircase is 2×11 steps.

8. What Month–I

February of a leap year. If a month starts and ends with the same day of the week, it must have a complete number of weeks plus one more day. The only possible month is a 29-day February.

9. What Month—II

August. In order to add up to 38, it can only be the highest possible number for the last Monday of a month (31) and the highest for the first Thursday of a month (7). Therefore, both last month and the current must have 31 days. The only two 31-day months in a row in the same calendar year are July and August.

10. Eve's Enigma

Thursday. The snake is lying, because it says that today is Saturday and tomorrow is Wednesday. Therefore, today is one of the days when the snake lies (Tuesday, Thursday, and Saturday). It cannot be Saturday or else the snake would not be lying in one statement. Nor can it be Tuesday, for the same reason. It can only be Thursday.

11. Soccer Scores—I

The Eagles had 5 points. There were 10 matches in the tournament with a total of 20 points to be won by the teams. The table already has 15 points assigned. Therefore, the remaining 5 points must belong to the Eagles.

12. Soccer Scores—II

Lions 0, Tigers 0. Lions 1, Bears 0. Tigers 1, Bears 1. The Lions could only win 3 points by winning one match and tying another. Since they only scored one goal, the results must be 1–0 and 0–0. The Bears tied one and lost the other match. The scores must have been 1–1 and 0–1. Their tied game must have been against the Tigers. So the Lions beat the Bears 1–0, and the Lions tied the Tigers 0–0.

13. What Time Is It—I

5:00. From here, the minute hand will take 30 minutes to reach 6, and the hour hand will take an entire hour.

14. What Time Is It—II

There are two possible times in this situation: 5:15 (the minute hand takes 15 minutes to reach 6 and the hour hand takes 45) and 3:45 (the minute hand takes 45 minutes to reach 6 and the hour hand takes 2 hours and 15 minutes, which is 135 minutes).

15. What Time Is It—III

2:12. The hour hand is at the first minute mark after 2, and the minute hand is on the next minute mark.

16. What Time Is It—IV

9:48. The minute hand is on 48 minutes and the hour hand is on the next minute mark.

17. Prohibited Connection

Each middle digit (2, 3, 4, and 5) can only be connected to three others (for example, 2 can only be connected to 4, 5, and 6). There are two circles with four connections. We can only put 1 and 6 in them. Once you insert these, the rest is easy to figure out. Another solution exists where the order of the numbers is switched, so 1 and 6 switch, as do 2 and 5, and 3 and 4.

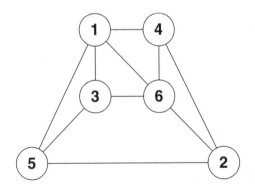

18. Concentric

30 square inches. We turn the small square as shown in the picture on the next page. We can see that it is half the size of the big one, as indicated by the dotted lines. These dotted lines divide the large square into 8 triangles, and the small square into 4 triangles.

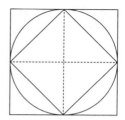

19. John Cash

The reward was 125 dollars. If you erase 1, you have 25 left, which is one fifth the original amount. If you erase 2, you have 5 left, which is one fifth of this amount.

To get 125, find a two-digit number in which you can take the first digit off and the result is one fifth of the number. The only possible number is 25. $25 \times 5 = 125$.

20. Russian Roulette

The arsenic is in the jar labeled "SUGAR." We know that the snuff is above the salt. The arsenic cannot be on the right side, because then the salt would be in the jar labeled "SALT." It cannot be in the center either, because then the second answer would not be true since the coffee and sugar would not be next to each other. Therefore, it is on the left. So the coffee and sugar are in the jars marked "TEA" and "SALT," respectively, leaving arsenic for either the jar marked "ARSENIC" or "SUGAR." Since it's not in the correctly labeled jar, it must be in the jar marked "SUGAR," and the tea is in the jar marked "ARSENIC."

21. New Race

One car goes twice as fast as the other. The first crossing took place at point A. Consider A as a new starting point. Do the same for every crossing point. Since they drive at consistent speeds, the distances from A to B, B to C, and C to A are the same. After point A, one car must drive twice the distance as the other to reach B at the same time. Therefore, one goes twice as fast as the other.

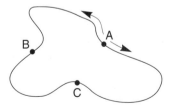

22. Nice Discounts

You first buy books for $80 and, the next day, for $70, which represents a discount of $70 × .08 = $5.60. (It will be the same result by inverting the order of the purchases, first the $70 purchase and the next day the $80 one.)

23. The Calculator Keys

There are two possibilities:
  1. Change the 4 with the 5 and the 2 with the 8. 729 – 546 = 183.
  2. Change the 3 with the 9 and the 4 with the 6. 783 – 654 = 129.

24. Enigmatic Fares

98999 and 99000. The tickets are consecutive in number. If the professor had answered "yes" to the question about the five digits of one ticket adding up to 35, the friend could have not figured out the numbers. There would have been several possibilities (78659 and 78660, 36989 and 36990, etc.), so the professor must have answered that indeed none of the tickets added up to 35.

Both tickets add up to 62 (an even number), which means that the first one must end in a 9. If it ended in only one 9, one ticket would add up to 35. Let's call the first ticket ABCD9 and the second one ABC(D + 1)0. The sum is A + B + C + D + 9 + A + B + C + D + 1 = 62, meaning that A + B + C + D + 9 = 35. If it ended in two 9s, the sum of both tickets would give us an odd number.

Therefore, the ticket must end in three 9s and no more than three, or the sum wouldn't be 62. We can call the tickets AB999 and A(B+1)000, where B is not 9. The sum of both is $2 \times (A + B) + 28 = 62$. Therefore, A = 9 and B = 8.

25. Horoscope

The teacher is a Pisces. This conversation could have only taken place on February 29. She was 29 then. Six days later (March 6), having turned 30, it becomes true that the date is one fifth of her age. This means her birthday occurs during the six first days of March.

26. Strangers in the Night

The blonde woman killed Mr. Farnanski. There are only four true statements. Only one person is guilty. Therefore, three of the "I'm innocent" statements are true. Only one more statement can be true, and this must be the one made by the man in the dark suit or by the blonde woman. Therefore, "The brunette killed him" and "One of the men killed him" are false statements, so the blonde woman is the killer.

27. The Foreigners and the Menu

They could have ordered ABCDD their first night (finding out what D is), AEFGG the second night (finding out what G is and what A is, since they had ordered it the previous night, too), and BEHII the third night, (finding out what I, B, and E are). This leaves C, F, and H out, and since they had never ordered these dishes twice and each came on a different night, they should know what they are.

28. Monte Carlo

He lost. Every time that Hystrix wins, his money increases 1.5 times (with $100, he bets $50 and if he wins, he has $150). When he loses, his money is reduced by half. So a win-loss combination results in a loss of one quarter of his money. The more he plays, the more money he loses, even though he wins the same number of times as he loses.

29. The Harem

There were seven locks. Let's name the locks A, B, C, D, E, F, and G. The vizier had keys for A, B, C, D, E, and F. One of the slaves had the keys for A, B, C, and G. Another one, for A, D, E, and G. Another, for B, D, F, and G. And the last, for C, E, F, and G. With seven locks, the Great Tamerlan's system works—but not with fewer locks.

30. The Dividing End

The number is 381654729.

If the number is ABCDEFGHI, B, D, F, and H are even numbers. The rest are odd numbers. ABCDE can be divided evenly by 5, thus E = 5.

ABCD can be divided evenly by 4. Therefore, CD can also be divided evenly by 4, and since C is an odd number, D can only be 2 or 6.

ABCDEF can be divided evenly by 6 (by 2 and by 3). Since ABC can be divided by 3, DEF can be also. Consequently, DEF is 258 or 654.

You can deduce the rest from here.

31. A Warm Farewell

10 men and 6 women. The number of handshakes and kisses adds up to 55. Each Porter says good-bye to each Robinson. If we multiply the number of members of both families, the result should be 55. There are two possibilities: 55 = 11 × 5 (one family with 11 members and the other one with 5), or 55

$= 55 \times 1$ (which could not be possible, since a family is not formed by only one person).

We now analyze the handshakes following the same procedure. There are two possibilities: $21 = 7 \times 3$ (7 men in one family and 3 in the other) or $21 = 21 \times 1$ (which could not be possible, because none of these families has so many members, as seen above). Therefore, one family is formed by 7 men and 4 women, and the other by 3 men and 2 women.

32. Added Corners

The 8 cannot be in a corner, so we have to put it in a square. The 7 must go in a square too. This makes it easy to figure out the rest.

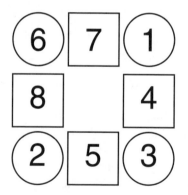

33. Logic Apples

Alonso 1, Bertrand 2, George 3, and Kurt 5.

Alonso could not have eaten 5 or more. Bertrand could not have eaten only one or he would have known that he hadn't eaten more than Alonso. Neither could he have eaten 5 or more. He could have eaten 2, 3, or 4. George figures this out, although he still doesn't know if he ate more than Bertrand. This means that George must have eaten 3 or 4. Kurt can only deduce the other amounts if he ate 5. And the rest, in order to add up to 11, must have eaten 1, 2, and 3.

34. The Island and the Englishmen

Six Englishmen. Let's draw four circles representing the clubs. Every two clubs have one member in common, so we draw a line from each circle to one point (an Englishman). Each dot is connected to two lines. This is the situation in the illustration, indicating six Englishmen.

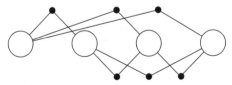

35. Rectangles

Both rectangles have the same area, 40 square inches. If you draw the dotted line you will see that the line divides the inclined figure into two equal pairs of triangles on both sides.

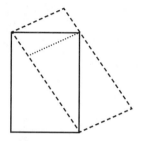

36. On the Route of Marco Polo

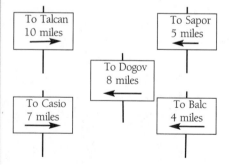

The road signs each point to a different village. The sum of distances in one direction and the sum in the opposite direction must be equal. This can only be achieved with $10 + 7 = 8 + 5 + 4$. Therefore, the signs with 10 and 7 point in one direction and the three others point in the opposite direction.

37. Touching Squares

14 squares.

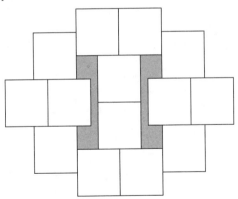

38. Blood and Sand

Lincoln Dustin died at 5:30. At first the commissioner thought that Mr. Dustin had inverted the hourglass at 7:30 (which would account for the 15 hours that the hourglass took to finish). The evident suspect is Begonias, who was at the mansion at the time. Then Begonias told him that he had inverted the hourglass. This made the commissioner think that Mr. Dustin had inverted the hourglass and then Begonias did as well, which means that the time between both inversions counted twice toward the total amount of time. Since the total time was 3 hours, Begonias inverted the hourglass one and a half hours after Mr. Dustin had. If Begonias said that he had inverted it at 7 P.M., this means that Mr. Dustin inverted it at 5:30.

39. Equal Vision

Six watchmen. One way to do it is shown below.

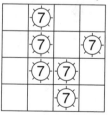

40. Mister Digit Face

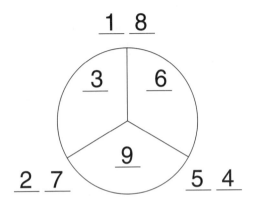

The 9 must be inside the circle, because no product can be 9_ or _9. The 1, 2, and 5 must be outside the circle. From here on you can find the solution. (Other answers can be made by flipping or rotating the circle.)

41. Digit Tree

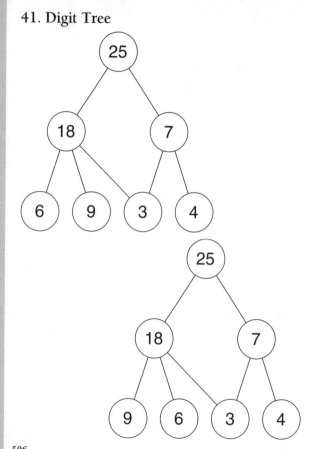

42. Segments

4	7	2	9	1	8	3	6	5

The numbers 4 and 5 must be at both ends because the sum of the nine digits is 45. Then we place 3 and 6, then 2 and 7, and finally 1, 8, and 9. (The order of the numbers can be reversed.)

43. International Summit

A-Spanish, French, Portuguese; B-all; C-all except French; D-Spanish; and E-French and Italian.

Draw a table with five rows and five columns, making the languages the column headers and the people the row headers. Statement 1 tells us that B and C speak English. Mark an X in the corresponding cells. Statement 1 also tells us that D does not speak English. Mark a zero in the corresponding cell. Additionally, statement 1 tells us B, C, and D speak Spanish. Mark it in the table. Follow the same procedure for statement 2 and statement 3. Statement 3 explains that the only common language to C and E is Italian, and since C also speaks English and Spanish, we can write zeroes for E in those columns.

In a similar way, write a zero for French in C.
This is how the table will look at this point:

	Eng.	Sp.	Fr.	Port.	Ital.
A			X		
B	X	X	X		
C	X	X	O		X
D	O	X			
E	O	O	X		X

We can see that three people speak Spanish and French. Add another X for Spanish, since it is the most common language.

From statement 6 we need one person who speaks only one language. The only possibility is D. Complete the row with zeroes. From statement 4 we look for the three people who speak Portuguese. They cannot be C and E, since their common language was Italian. Therefore, two of the Portuguese speakers must be A and B. From statement 6 we need a person who speaks only two languages. It can only be E, so we write a zero for E in Portuguese. The third person who speaks Portuguese must be C, so we mark an X in the corresponding cell. We look now for the person who speaks three languages, and it can only be A. Fill in the row with zeroes. So, the person who speaks five languages is B. The table is now complete.

44. Earthlings

Uruguay came in first, Spain second, Zaire third. The second earthling has one answer in common with the first one and one in common with the third one. In which category is the second earthling, then? He cannot always be telling the truth, because he has something in common with a liar, and he cannot always be lying because he has something in common with the honest one. If his first answer were true, then the third one would also be true, and they would be the same as the first and third answers from the honest man. There is no match, however, so this is not the case.

Therefore, the first answer from the man that alternately lies and tells the truth must be a lie. The second is true and the third a lie, so the third man is the honest one, and thus his answers are the results of the soccer championship.

INDEX

Key: puzzle, *hint*, **answer**

Brain Bafflers, 255–274, **444–452**

Checker Puzzles, 219–254, *385–386*, **430–443**

Crosswords, 177–217, **420–429**

Cryptic Crosswords, 43–83, **396–405**

Crypto-Quotes, 133–176, *383–384*, **407–419**

Hard-to-Solve Brainteasers, 349–380, **489–509**

Mind Bogglers, 7–42, **388–395**

Puzzles for Word Lovers, 275–313, **453–472**

Quick-to-Solve Brainteasers, 315–347, **473–488**

Rhyming Picture Puzzles, 85–132, *382*, **406**

WHAT IS AMERICAN MENSA?

American Mensa
The High IQ Society
One out of 50 people qualifies
for American Mensa ...
Are YOU the One?

American Mensa, Ltd. is an organization for individuals who have one common trait: a score in the top two percent of the population on a standardized intelligence test. Over five million Americans are eligible for membership ... you may be one of them.

• **Looking for intellectual stimulation?**
You'll find a good "mental workout" in the *Mensa Bulletin*, our national magazine. Voice your opinion in the newsletter published by your local group. And attend activities and gatherings with fascinating programs and engaging conversation.

• **Looking for social interaction?**
There's something happening on the Mensa calendar almost daily. These range from lectures to game nights to parties. Each year, there are over 40 regional gatherings

and the Annual Gathering, where you can meet people, exchange ideas, and make interesting new friends.

• **Looking for others who share your special interest?** Whether your interest might be in computer gaming, Monty Python, or scuba, there's probably a Mensa Special Interest Group (SIG) for you. There are over 150 SIGs, which are started and maintained by members.

So contact us to receive a free brochure and application.

> **American Mensa, Ltd.**
> **1229 Corporate Drive West**
> **Arlington, TX 76006**
> **(800) 66-MENSA**
> **AmericanMensa@compuserve.com**
> **http://www.us.mensa.org**

In Canada, contact:

> **Mensa Canada**
> 329 March Road, Suite 232, Box 11
> Kanata, Ontario Canada K2K 2E1
> (613) 599-5897 info@canada.mensa.org

If you don't live in the United States or Canada and would like to get in touch with your national Mensa, contact:

> **Mensa International**
> 15 The Ivories
> 6-8 Northampton Street, Islington
> London N1 2HY England